Hidden Truths of Revelation

To Rebecca,
Thank you for all your help in getting this Book out. God Bless You
Adrian

Hidden Truths
of
Revelation

Adrian Marine

Copyright © 2007 by Adrian Marine.

Library of Congress Control Number: 2007900161
ISBN: Hardcover   978-1-4257-5245-3
        Softcover   978-1-4257-5244-6

All rights reserved. No part of this book may be reproduced or transmitted in any form or by any means, electronic or mechanical, including photocopying, recording, or by any information storage and retrieval system, without permission in writing from the copyright owner.

This book was printed in the United States of America.

To order additional copies of this book, contact:
Xlibris Corporation
1-888-795-4274
www.Xlibris.com
Orders@Xlibris.com
37143

Contents

Acknowledgments 9
Introduction 11

PART 1: THINGS PAST—VIEW OF HEAVEN

Chapter 1   Jesus's Vision to John 15

PART 2: THINGS NOW—IN THE FIRST CENTURY

Chapter 2   Epistle to Four Churches 21
Chapter 3   Epistle to Three Churches......................... 27

PART 3: THE BEGINNING OF THE VISIONS OF THE FUTURE

Chapter 4   The Throne of God in Heaven 35
Chapter 5   Jesus Steps Before God in Heaven............. 39
Chapter 6   Six Seals: An Overview of the Tribulation 42
Chapter 7   The 144,000 and the Tribulation Saints..... 47

PART 4: THE FIRST HALF OF THE TRIBULATION

Chapter 8   The Tribulation Begins 53
Chapter 9   Woe, Woe, Woe: More Trumpets............... 55
Chapter 10   The Seven Thunders.................................. 59
Chapter 11   The Seventh Trumpet 61
Chapter 12   Satan the Destroyer Comes to Earth 65

PART 5: THE SECOND HALF OF THE TRIBULATION

Chapter 13   The Beast and the False Prophet (666)....... 73
Chapter 14   The Seven Voices from Heaven.................. 81
Chapter 15   The Saints Are All in Heaven..................... 87

Chapter 16　　　　The Wrath of God 89

PART 6: A REVIEW OF BABYLON'S DESTRUCTION

Chapter 17　　　　The Harlot and the Beast 97
Chapter 18　　　　Babylon the Great 101

PART 7: THE SECOND COMING AND NEW AGES

Chapter 19　　　　The Return of Christ 107
Chapter 20　　　　The Millennium and the Judgment 113
Chapter 21　　　　A New Heaven and New Earth 118
Chapter 22　　　　Inside Our New Home 122

Conclusion 127

Bibliography 135

List of Photographs and Charts

<u>Michael the Archangel throwing Satan out of Heaven</u> (Rev. 12). This cover is a photograph of a large ancient painting taken at St. Peter's Church in Joppa, Israel, in 2006.

<u>Chart 1</u> (Rev. 8). This is an overview of the seven-year tribulation.

<u>Temple Mount</u> (Rev. 11). This is where the two witnesses will help rebuild the Jewish temple. This photograph was taken in Jerusalem, Israel, in 2006.

<u>Mary with the Twelve Stars</u> (Rev. 12). The woman and the twelve stars represent Israel who flees from the Antichrist. This photograph was taken in the center of Jerusalem, Israel, in 2006.

<u>The Beast</u> (Rev. 13). The beast and the false prophet will rule from the Temple Mount during the last three and a half years of the tribulation. This sinister-looking image is actually a large slab of marble at the entrance of the Dome of the Rock on the Temple Mount. It is about eight feet tall. This photograph was taken in Jerusalem, Israel, in 2006.

<u>The Beast—Close-up</u> (Rev. 13). This photograph is a close-up of the image shown above.

<u>Chart 2</u> (Rev. 14) This is an overview of the last three and a half years of the tribulation called the Great Tribulation.

The Valley of Megiddo (Rev. 19). The battle of Armageddon will take place in this valley. This photograph was taken at the southern end of the Valley of Megiddo in Israel in 2006.

The Mount of Olives (Rev. 20). Jesus will return to the Mount of Olives at His Second Coming. This photograph was taken in Jerusalem, Israel, in 2006.

Acknowledgments

After working for eight years on this book, I would like to thank all of the people who helped in any way to get this book published. I would like to say thank you to my family, friends, and associates who encouraged me to finish this book, especially those in my Revelation Bible studies.

I would like to offer special thanks to

- the guys in my Promise Keepers Bible study group (Ben, Don, Bill, John, and Dale) who were willing to sit through a full one-year Bible study on the book of Revelation and helped me edit my notes when I first started writing this book;
- the ladies at Rainbow Fire Camp who always wanted to read the chapters of my book at lunch and quizzed me on the meaning of the verses as I was writing this book;
- David, my longtime friend who was always willing to listen and debate with me over the meanings of the many words and verses in Revelation;
- the Christian Writers Guild in Temecula that helped me to rewrite parts of my book;
- and my wife, Leslie, whom I could never thank enough for all the endless hours of work that she put into this book. Without her help, patience, and encouragement, this work would never have been finished.

May God bless you all!

Introduction

When I was at my doctor's office for a physical he asked me what I was doing with myself now that I am retired from the fire department. I told him that I was getting ready to publish a book on Revelation. He then asked me if I had a degree or had taken any classes in theology. I explained that while I did not have any fancy titles or degrees, I have been diligently studying the Bible on the end-times for over thirty-five years, and I have read hundreds of books and articles on the subject.

Since I became a born-again Christian in 1971, I have been fascinated with the Bible and its teaching on the end-times. But the more I read, studied, and listened about the end-times and the book of Revelation, the more I realized that many of the teachings did not harmonize with the Bible and the historical writings of the early church fathers. In 1998, I started teaching a Bible study on Revelation to a group of my friends at Promise Keepers. As I studied for the lessons, God began to open my eyes to some of His truths through revelations and scriptures. Then, through the urging of many friends and associates, my notes from that class became the basis for this book.

After I completed the manuscript for this book, I came across three other authors with similar views as mine (Marvin Rosenthal, *The Pre-wrath Rapture of the Church*, 1990; Robert Van Kampen, *The Sign,* 1992; and Jack Hayford, *E-Quake*, 1999). I discovered that my view on the rapture was called "the prewrath rapture view."

I wrote this book to be a guide to understanding the book of Revelation and to help readers learn some of its hidden mysteries. I hope it can help all those who are searching for the truth and don't want to be confused anymore about the timing of the rapture and other end-times events.

The Seven Major Groups of Messages to Christians

The Letters to the Seven Churches	Chapters 2 + 3
The Seven Seals	Chapters 6 + 8
The Seven Trumpets	Chapters 8, 9 + 11
The Seven Thunders	Chapter 10
The Seven Types of Voices from Heaven	Chapter 14
The Seven Bowls of the Wrath of God	Chapter 16
The Seven Blessings	Page 133

PART 1

THINGS PAST—
VIEW OF HEAVEN

Chapter 1

Jesus's Vision to John

The Revelation of Jesus Christ, which God gave Him to show to His bond-servants, the things which must shortly take place. (Rev. 1:1)

John wrote the book of Revelation on the Island of Patmos about AD 96. He was told to write down the visions that he was about to see and to send them to the seven churches in Asia Minor (Turkey).

A Blessing

Blessed is he who reads and those who hear the words of this prophesy, and heed the things which are written in it; for the time is near. (Rev. 1:3)

Here we are promised a blessing if we read this book, or even hear its words, and heed them. Many churches today do not teach about the things written in the book of Revelation. They are missing a great blessing and can easily be led away from the truth of God's word by false teachers (2 Pet. 2:1).

When I was in high school over thirty years ago and going to the Catholic Church, I do not remember being taught much of anything about the return of Jesus Christ. I was only told that He was going to return, but that it was going to be somewhere at the end of time for the final judgment. During my junior year of high school, I received an invitation from a friend to attend a Campus Crusade for Christ youth rally. I learned at the rally that night that Jesus Christ could return soon! The Bible teacher shared the scriptures from the Bible as proof that we could be in the last days. I was blessed and alarmed at the same time. Jesus Christ was returning to earth, and we might see it. Wow! I started to read my family Bible and research the scriptures that were given that night. I asked my friend Karen if there were any books about the return of Jesus Christ to earth. She loaned me two books about the last days (*666* by Salem Kirban and *The Late Great Planet Earth* by Hal Lindsey). Soon after reading these books, I received a blessing by becoming a born-again Catholic and Christian! From this point of my life, I have been studying, praying, and listening to what the Lord could teach me about the end-times, which led to the writing of this book.

Jesus Christ

> *And from Jesus Christ, the faithful witness, the firstborn of the dead, and the ruler of the kings of the earth. To Him who loves us and released us from our sins by His blood - and He has made us to be a kingdom, priests to His God and Father - to Him be the glory and the dominion forever and ever. Amen. Behold, He is coming in the clouds, and every eye will see Him, even those who pierced Him; and all the tribes of the earth will mourn over Him. Sot it is to be. Amen. (Rev. 1:5-7)*

In these verses, John was speaking about Jesus Christ. They were written to build up our faith and to help us trust that Jesus gave him this vision. Also, John wanted us to know that when Jesus Christ returns, everyone on earth, past and present, will see His return. Jesus Christ's Second Coming is not something that happened about two thousand years ago, as many liberal scholars teach. He has not returned spiritually as some false teachers would have you believe, such as the Jehovah's Witnesses or the Seventh-day Adventists.

The Visions of the Past

> *I John, your brother and fellow partaker in the tribulation, . . . I was in the Spirit on the Lord's day, and I heard behind me a loud voice like the sound of a trumpet, saying, "Write in a book what you see . . ." (Rev. 1:9a-11a)*

John was filled with the Holy Spirit when he saw these visions back in AD 96. This chapter tells what John saw while he was in heaven with the Holy Spirit. It is a short chapter, but it is the introduction to the book of Revelation. John was ordered to write down the visions that he saw so that anyone reading them would receive a blessing; and that we, and the seven churches of Revelation, would be ready for His coming.

John's View of Jesus

We can see Jesus as He was in heaven, just as when John saw Him two thousand years ago in verses 10-18. This exalted view of Jesus is just like Daniel's vision in the Old Testament (Dan. 7:9; 10:5-6). Jesus is our hope for an everlasting life because He was raised from death and He has the keys to life. If we read the book of Revelation, He has promised that we will be blessed; and we should never be afraid to ask questions about its meaning. "*Do not be afraid; I am the first and the last . . .*" (Rev. 1:17b).

Three Main Parts of Revelation

> *Write therefore the things which you have seen, and the things which are, and the things which shall take place after these things. (Rev. 1:19)*

Here, the apostle was told that the book of Revelation would be divided into three main parts:

1. Past—John was told to write down the visions he had seen in the past, which is chapter 1.
2. Present—In chapters 2 and 3, John writes to the seven churches and tells them what they are doing wrong during their time, the first century.
3. Future—In chapters 4 to 22, John warns the seven churches of the things that will take place in the future.

PART 2

THINGS NOW—
IN THE FIRST CENTURY

Chapter 2

Epistle to Four Churches

Write therefore . . . the things which are . . . (Rev. 1:19a)

John writes this letter to the seven churches, which are in Asia Minor (Turkey). There were many other churches in Turkey at this time, but the reason that Jesus chose to have John write to these seven churches appears to be spiritual, like the number seven. These epistles, or letters, were written to those churches; but they were also written to be a guide to all Christians of all ages.

As you read the next two chapters in Revelation, the condemnations and the praises given to these churches by Jesus should move your heart. His message still applies to us today—to endure and not to grow weary.

The Church of Ephesus

But I have this against you, that you have left your first love. (Rev. 2:4)

Around AD 60, Paul the apostle wrote a letter to the city of Ephesus and prayed that Christ would give them both a revelation and wisdom (Eph. 1:15-17). Jesus answered Paul's prayer about thirty-six years later with this letter in Revelations 2:1-7. This short letter has seven commendations and only one reprimand.

Ephesus is located on the west coast of Turkey, about fifty miles south of the large city of Izmar. It was built at the mouth of the Cayster River, which is next to the Aegean Sea. Today the city is called Ephesus (or Efes), and there are many beautiful ruins from John's era that can be seen there.

Codrus, the last king of Athens, founded Ephesus about one thousand years before Christ. It was the fourth largest city in the Roman Empire with a population of over three hundred thousand. The Temple of Artemis (Diana) is located in the city of Ephesus, which is one of the Seven Wonders of the World. It is bigger and more beautiful than the Parthenon in Athens, Greece.

When Paul came to the city of Ephesus to preach, he ran into a lot of opposition from the Jews and the city merchants who made their living from selling many idols, which Paul preached against. Also, the merchants were going through a financially tough time because their harbor was silting up. Today, the harbor is about five miles from the coast.

I know your deeds and your toil and perseverance and that you can't endure evil men. (Rev. 2:2)

As Paul preached the Gospel, many Jews and Greeks in Ephesus were becoming Christians because of the power of the Holy Spirit. Pretty soon the whole city of Ephesus was seeing the works and deeds of these new Christians—prophesying, speaking in tongues, healing of the sick, confessing, and so forth (Acts 19:1-20). Another work that these Christians did was to build four large pillars in honor of the writers of the four Gospels and had their names carved into them. One of those pillars is still standing today in the ruins at Ephesus.

"But I have this against you, that you have left your first love" (Rev. 2:4).

This is the Lord's reprimand to the Christians in Ephesus and to many of us Christians today! When we first become Christians, we are on fire for the Lord; and we do many good deeds—we read our Bibles often, pray in the spirit, go to church, help those in need, and often seem to glow with excitement. But as the weeks, months, and years go by, we tend to lose that fire. For this reason it says, *"Awake, sleeper, and arise from the dead, and Christ will shine on you" (Eph. 5:14)*. Jesus Christ loved the church in Ephesus, and He loves us today. So, He warns us from heaven, *"Remember therefore from where you have fallen, and repent and do the deeds you did at first" (Rev. 2:5a)*.

The Church of Smyrna

> *I know your tribulation . . . but you are rich. (Rev. 2:9a)*

Smyrna (Izmir) is located in Turkey on the Aegean Sea. It was built next to the bay of Smyrna, on the acropolis of Mount Pagos, which is between the cities of Pergamos and Ephesus. Smyrna was an ancient Greek city that was destroyed around 600 BC, but it was refounded in 290 BC because of its well-protected harbor. Smyrna was a religious city that worshiped the Caesars and Rome. It became the main shipping and commercial center when the harbor in Ephesus silted up. Today, Smyrna is the beautiful port city of Izmir with a population of over three million.

In John's day, the city of Smyrna was the crown jewel of all the cities on the Mediterranean because of its beauty, wealth, weather, and commerce. Yet Christians found it very difficult to find work and live there because of persecution for their faith by the Jews and Romans. Christ warned the church of a coming tribulation in the following verse when he said, *"Do not fear what you are about to suffer . . . you may be tested, and you will have tribulation ten days" (Rev. 2:10)*.

These Christians were not raptured out of the earth before their tribulation but were told to remain faithful. We need to follow Christ's exhortation here and remain faithful during the coming tribulation. Polycarp, the great evangelist and bishop of Smyrna and a student of the apostle John, was burned alive for his faith in AD 166. Polycarp and the Christians of his day believed that they were going to go through the tribulation and knew the following verse, *"Be faithful until death, and I will give you the crown of life. He who has an ear, let Him hear what the Spirit says to the Churches" (Rev. 2:10b-11)*.

The Church of Pergamum

> *But I have a few things against you, because you . . . eat things sacrificed to idols, and commit acts of immorality [fornication]. (Rev. 2:14)*

Pergamum, or Pergamus as it is often called, is located fifty miles north of the city of Izmir (Smyrna). Pergamus was built on a beautiful acropolis overlooking two flowing rivers, about fifteen miles from the coast. Today, the small town of Bergama surrounds the ruins of Pergamus.

Pergamus was an ancient Anatolian settlement that became a major capital in that region under General Lysimachus in about 350 BC. The city's population grew to about one hundred thousand: and it had the largest library in the world (with over two hundred thousand volumes) until Marc Anthony gave most of the books to Cleopatra, the princess of Egypt. Later, under Eumences, a school of grammatical study and psychology was started.

"I know where you dwell, where Satan's throne is . . . where Satan dwells . . ." (Rev. 2:13).

To me, verse 13 means exactly what it says; and it is not a metaphor. Satan probably lived on this beautiful fortified acropolis, influencing the kings of Greece and later the Roman emperors who vacationed there. You can really see the handiwork of Satan there—world domination, open sexual lifestyle, sensual art, drunkenness, slavery, persecution, and killing of Christians. Also, look at the many temples to gods. Satan had set it up to get the whole world involved in idolatry:

- Dionysus—the half-man, half-goat god of wine who had two horns, hoofed feet, goatee, and a tail. He also seduces women with his flute.
- Asklepios—the snake god of healing.
- Artemis—(Diana) woman god with many breasts that could help you with sexual problems, or you could go to the temple prostitutes for help.
- Athena—the Maid of Athens that was a fearless warrior.
- Zeus—king of the gods. The largest sacrificial altar ever built was in this temple. It was later moved to the Berlin Museum in 1871, along with a large statue of Asklepios. Look what happened to Germany!

Repent therefore; or else I am coming to you quickly, and I will make war against them with the sword of My mouth (Rev. 2:16).

In this letter to the Christian church in Pergamus, Jesus warns them to stop committing fornication and to stop eating food sacrificed to idols, like the deities we saw above. This was difficult for them to do because everyone was having premarital sex, and so forth, just like they do today. Also, they were intermarrying with the non-Christians, as Balaam had encouraged the Israelites to do in the Old Testament. The Nicolaitans in verse 15 were probably leaders in the Christian church who took the middle-of-the-road stance on idols and sex. As good Christians back then behaved, we also need to be holy. We are the salt of the earth and need to set an example to others; and if we are not walking in Him, we need to repent!

> *Therefore repent; or else I am coming to you quickly, and I will make war against them with the sword of My mouth. He who has an ear, let him hear what the Spirit says to the churches. (Rev. 2:16-17)*

The Church of Thyatira

> *You tolerate the woman Jezebel (Rev. 2:20a-b).*

Thyatira lies forty miles southeast of Pergamus on a small hill overlooking a valley that used to be a key trade route. Thyatira was founded in the third century before Christ by a Greek ruler named Seleucus I and used as a border outpost. Today, the town is called Akhisar; and there is very little left of its ruins.

> *I know your deeds, and your love and faith and service and perseverance, and that your deeds of late are greater than at first. (Rev. 2:19)*

This sounds like a church most of us belong to now; but we know that there are no perfect churches out there.

> *But I have this against you, that you tolerate the women Jezebel, who calls herself a prophetess and she teaches and leads My bond-servants astray, so that they commit acts of immorality and eat things sacrificed to idols. (Rev. 2:20)*

It sounds like this prophetess Jezebel came from the city of Pergamus, and I believe this message applies to many of our churches today. With all of the pornography on TV, movies, magazines, and radio, it is no wonder many of our fellow Christians and kids are starting to lose their morals. Today, many of our ministers and priests are like Jezebel because they teach that it is all right to practice homosexuality, adultery, idolatry, and even to get married to people that practice or believe in these acts.

> *And I gave her time to repent; and she does not want to repent of her immorality. Behold, I will cast her upon a bed of sickness, and those who commit adultery with her into great tribulation, unless they repent of her deeds. (Rev. 2:21, 22)*

The above verses are not talking about the end-times tribulation but about a wrath that was about to fall upon them in their time. Today, many of our church leaders are homosexuals and commit adultery; and we see the fruits of their beliefs—AIDS, abortions, herpes, TB, hepatitis, drug addictions, and so on. We are being cast upon a bed of sickness as Thyatira was.

> *But I say to you, the rest who are in Thyatira who do not hold this teaching . . .*
> *I place no other burden on you. (Rev. 2:24)*

Chapter 3

Epistle to Three Churches

The Church of Sardis

Wake up . . . for I have not found your deeds completed in the sight of God (Rev. 3:2).

Sardis is located about thirty-five miles southeast of Thyatira on the slopes of Mount Timolus, next to the river called Pactohus. Today, the town of Sart sits at the base of the beautiful acropolis where Sardis was located.

Sardis was founded over a thousand years before Christ and was the ancient capital of Lydia. Sardis was built on a 1,500-foot citadel that was almost impossible to climb on three sides. This made it a perfect location for a fort. In about 556 BC, King Croesus decided to modernize Sardis and make it into one of the most beautiful cities in the world. He built large marble buildings, put up walls, set up public works, and placed beautiful statues throughout the city. Sardis became a very rich city because of its gold mines, fertile valleys, and trade.

I know your deeds, that you have a name that you are alive, but you are dead. (Rev. 3:1b)

What does Jesus mean when He says, "You are alive, but you are dead"? When Jesus says you are dead, believe me, you are dead. You are not going to heaven. Many people think that when you go to church on Sunday, lead church studies, or wear a large cross or even holy robes, you are a true Christian going to heaven. Look what Jesus said about this in the Gospel.

> *Woe to you, scribes and Pharisees, hypocrites! For you are like whitewashed tombs which on the outside appear beautiful, but inside they are full of dead men's bones and uncleanness. Even so you too outwardly appear righteous to men, but inwardly you are full of hypocrisy and lawlessness. (Matt. 23:27-28)*

James, the brother of Jesus, said, *"Faith, if it has no works, is dead" (James 2:17)*. Jesus gave us a great example of good works in His parable of the good Samaritan in the Gospel of Luke, chapter 10. Many in the church of Sardis appear to have lost that spirit of love and mercy that comes in knowing Christ.

> *So remember therefore what you have received and heard; and keep it, and repent. (Rev. 3:3a-b)*

Paul says that the blood of Christ, through the eternal Spirit, will cleanse your conscience of dead works (Heb. 9:14). And he said not to be conformed to this world but to be transformed by the renewing of your mind, that you may prove what the will of God is (Rom. 12:2). If we repent, He is faithful to forgive us of our sins.

> *But you have a few people in Sardis who have not soiled their garments; and they will walk with Me. (Rev. 3:4a-c)*

These Christians in Sardis knew what the will of God was and were walking in Him, and will walk with Him in the new heaven and new earth. James tells us what true religion is in James 1: 27:

- To visit orphans in distress
- To visit widows in distress
- To keep oneself unstained by the world

The deeds of most of the church of Sardis were empty words, and they needed to wake up and repent or they would die.

The Church of Philadelphia

Because you have kept the word of My perseverance. (Rev. 3:10a)

Philadelphia sits about thirty miles inland from Sardis, in a very beautiful valley next to the Cogamus River and is called Alasehir. Attalus II, king of Pergamus, founded the city in about 150 BC. Attalus II built the city for his brother, whom he greatly loved; and this is where we get the expression "city of brotherly love." Philadelphia was one of the last cities in Turkey to resist the Muslim invaders.

He who is holy, who is true, who has the key of David, who opens and no one will shut, and who shuts and no one opens. (Rev. 3:7b)

Philadelphia and Smyrna were the only two churches that escaped criticism in the book of Revelation. They were faithful churches that Jesus promised to bless and give a crown to when He opened the doors of heaven to them. Jesus is the door to heaven and has the key of David (Isa. 22:22-23 and Luke 1:32). No pope, church, prophet, or person can claim to be the only way to heaven because Jesus is the only way to salvation; and these two churches are our example because they kept the word.

Because you have kept the word of My perseverance, I also will keep you from the hour of testing, that hour which is about to come upon the whole world, to test those who dwell upon the whole earth. (Rev. 3:10)

This verse is most likely telling the Christians in Philadelphia that they are going to escape some of the persecution during the Great Tribulation. We may be rescued or raptured from the Antichrist before the wrath of God, which begins in Revelation chapter 16. Voices from heaven also warn us during the Great Tribulation in Revelation chapter 14 that the hour of wrath or judgment is about to happen.

and he said with a loud voice, "Fear God, and give Him glory, because the hour of His judgment has come; worship Him who made the heaven and the earth and sea and springs of waters." (Rev. 14:7)

This hour, in the second half of the tribulation, is when the whole world is tested; while in the first part of the tribulation, only parts of the world are tested. John thought he was in the last hour (1 John 2:18), but I believe that the last hour is in the second half of the tribulation.

> *But they receive authority as kings with the beast for one hour. (Rev. 17:12b)*

Scripture says we are not destined for wrath (1 Thess. 5: 9), but that wrath of God will not happen until He first rescues Israel, and then us.

> *And He who sat on the cloud swung His sickle over the earth; and the earth was reaped. (Rev. 14:16)*

This Scripture is like a riddle that tells us that we are going to be raptured from the earth before the wrath of God in chapter 16. Hallelujah to God, we miss His wrath!

> *I am coming quickly; hold fast what you have, in order that no one will take your crown. He who overcomes, I will make him a pillar in the temple of God. (Rev. 3:11-12a)*

The Church of Laodicea

> *So because you are lukewarm, and neither hot nor cold; I will spit you out of My mouth. (Rev. 3:16)*

Laodicea is located about 125 miles east of Ephesus on a small plateau next to the Lycus River. It is also located about twenty miles northwest of the ancient town of Colossae and six miles south of the thermal hot springs of Pamukkale, one of the natural wonders of Turkey. The Romans built a pipe to carry hot mineral water to Laodicea, but it is believed that the water was only lukewarm by the time it reached the city. Near the hot springs, Italian excavators have discovered the tomb of the apostle Phillip, who was martyred here in AD 80. Today, many of the ruins at Laodicea either have not been excavated or are poorly preserved; and the nearest modern city, Denizli, is located a few miles to the west.

Laodicea was refounded in 261 BC by King Antiochus and named after his sister Laodice. Laodicea was a very rich city that dealt in banking and commerce. It was a place of science, sports, literature, and Greek culture. It also had a medical school that was well known and developed an ointment for the eyes that was very popular, although it was useless.

> *Because you say, "I am rich, and have become wealthy, and have need of nothing," and you do not know that you are wretched and miserable and poor and blind and naked. I advise you to buy from me gold refined by fire, that you may become rich, and white garments, that you may clothe yourself, and that the shame of your nakedness may not be revealed; and eye salve to anoint your eyes, that you may see. (Rev. 3:17-18)*

Jesus loved the church at Laodicea but warned them that they were lukewarm in faith and works. You may ask, "What is wrong with being lukewarm?" Being lukewarm is like receiving a warm cup of coffee or soup on a cold day when you were expecting it to be delivered hot. It is disgusting and needs to be reheated or thrown out! Jesus said in verse 17 that lukewarm is being wretched, miserable, poor, naked, and blind.

> *I advise you to buy from Me gold refined by fire that you may become rich, and white garments, that you may clothe yourself, and that the shame of your nakedness may not be revealed; and eye salve to anoint your eyes, that you may see. (Rev. 3:18)*

Jesus warned us not to be lukewarm but to be on fire for the Lord! We are blind until the Holy Spirit comes into our heart and opens our eyes. Paul the apostle was blind spiritually and appeared wicked to God for killing Christians in the name of God. We are poor in the sight of God until we get a heart of gold and naked unless we are righteous in His sight. To become rich in the Lord, we need to attend a Bible-believing church where the Holy Spirit leads the preacher, as what Romans chapter 10 talks about.

> *So faith comes from hearing, and hearing the word of Christ. (Rom. 10:17)*

> *Those whom I love, I reprove and discipline; therefore be zealous and repent. Behold, I stand at the door and knock; if anyone hears My voice and opens the door, I will come in to him, and will dine with him, and he with Me. (Rev. 3:19-20)*

The Seven Churches in Time

The seven churches in Asia Minor are now gone. They are mostly ruins and are slowly being rebuilt as beautiful tourist spots. The same is true of the ruins in Athens and Rome. There are few Christian churches left in these ancient cities. The ones that are there are generally small because Turkey is mostly Moslem, and they do not tolerate Christian witnessing. Even in this new millennium, Turkish officials are harsh on the small Christian churches there by putting the members in jail for even singing in their churches.

The seven churches of Asia Minor were real churches in the first century that needed to be warned about the coming tribulation. Those warnings apply to us today just as the other letters to the churches in the New Testament apply to us today. Some Christian scholars teach that these seven churches represent seven ages of human history after the birth of Christ. One of the earliest scholars to come up with this idea was the Puritan John Bale (1495-1563). Today, many scholars and churches have set up timelines for the seven churches like the one below (all years are AD):

1. Ephesus 1-100
2. Smyrna 100-316
3. Pergamum 316-500
4. Thyatira 500-1500
5. Sardis 1500-1750
6. Philadelphia 1790-1910
7. Laodicea 1910-present

These timelines are an assumption, and they are FALSE because these warnings were written to the churches in the first century.

Everyone who hears the words of the prophecy of this book; if anyone adds to them, God shall add to him the plagues. (Rev. 22:18)

PART 3

THE BEGINNING OF THE VISIONS OF THE FUTURE

Chapter 4

The Throne of God in Heaven

In this chapter, John is taken to heaven in the spirit from his island prison of Patmos. From there, he sees a vision of heaven in the future where God is on His throne surrounded by a beautiful rainbow, twenty-four elders, and four awesome creatures. This chapter can be divided into five main parts:

1. John Is Taken to Heaven
2. God on the Throne
3. The Twenty-four Elders
4. The Seven Spirits of God
5. The Four Living Creatures

John Is Taken to Heaven

> After these things I looked, and behold, a door standing open in heaven, and the first voice which I had heard, like the sound of a trumpet speaking with me, said, "Come up here, and I will show you what must take place after these things. Immediately I was in the Spirit; and behold, a throne was standing in heaven and One sitting on the throne. (Rev. 4:1-2)

It is very evident what John is writing about here. After John writes the letters to the seven churches in chapters 2 and 3, a door of heaven is opened so that John can see the throne of God in heaven sometime in the future.

A voice like a trumpet tells John to come up here. It is not the Christian church that is taken up to heaven (raptured), as some writers would have you believe, but it is John. Also, John had to be taken up to heaven to see the visions of the future so that he might be able to write about them in this book of Revelation.

The Throne of God

> *And He who was sitting was like a jasper stone and a sardius in appearance; and there was a rainbow around the throne, like an emerald in appearance. (Rev. 4:3)*

This is an awesome thing, being able to go to heaven and see God on His throne. I don't know if John actually saw God here or just a vision of Him that is symbolized by two stones because no mortal man can see God and live (Ex. 33:20). But John was in the spirit at this time and not in his mortal body (see Job 19:25-26). Also, God is described here as two stones, which have been called by some teachers as the first and last stones found on the breast piece of judgment found in Exodus 28:15-20. Later in Revelation 20:11, John sees this great white throne, but it doesn't describe Him who sits on it.

The rainbow at the end of this verse appears to sparkle with the beauty of an emerald, and this rainbow forms a circle around the throne. When a rainbow is seen from the air today, it makes a full circle. This means the throne of God could be floating in heaven. My older brother, Tony, is a helicopter pilot. He has told me that when you see a rainbow from the sky, it makes a roll circle rather than an arch. So, John saw this vision before men knew that rainbows formed a circle when they are seen from the air! Praise God for this proof today that this vision to John is true!

The Twenty-four Elders

> *And around the throne were twenty-four thrones; and upon the thrones I saw twenty-four elders sitting, clothed in white garments, and golden crowns on their heads. And from the throne proceed flashes of lightning and sounds and peals of thunder. And there were seven lamps of fire burning before the throne, which were the seven Spirits of God; and before the throne there was, as it were, a sea of glass like crystal; and in the center and around the throne, four living creatures full of eyes in front and behind. (Rev. 4:4-6)*

When many people read this part of Revelation for the first time, they don't understand what John saw here and proceed to close their Bibles because it just doesn't make any sense to them. Throughout history, people have been trying to figure out what John saw here in heaven. Many Bible scholars spiritualize (guess at) the meaning of these visions because it makes their theories on what is going to happen in the future a lot more believable. Today, you can find examples of this type of spiritualizing of scripture in many Christian churches, books, and radio talk shows. For example, right here in Revelation 4:4, many Bible scholars believe that the twenty-four elders represent the Christian church in heaven after they get raptured out of the earth. I don't believe this big guess because John wrote that he was taken up to heaven and saw the twenty-four elders in heaven, not the raptured church. I believe that the twenty-four elders could be the twelve sons of Jacob and the twelve apostles of Jesus.

The Seven Spirits of God

In Revelation 4:5, John sees seven lamps of fire burning, which he says are the seven spirits of God, which he also saw in Revelation 1:4. Later in Revelation 3:1 and 5:6, John sees these same spirits with Jesus Christ; but this time, the seven spirits appear with horns and eyes. There is no explanation given as to why the Holy Spirit changes its appearance, but God doesn't always explain His ways.

> *After being baptized, Jesus came up immediately from the water; and behold, the heavens were opened, and he saw the Spirit of God descending as a dove and lighting on Him. (Matt. 3:16)*

The Four Living Creatures

In Revelation 4:6, 9, John sees four creatures around the throne of God. Who are these four creatures? These four living creatures appear to be some kind of angels because they have wings (six), and they are at the throne of God. The prophets Ezekiel (Ezek. 1:5-10) and Isaiah (Isa. 6:2) each had similar visions of these creatures or angels, which helps make Johns vision believable.

> *And the first creature was like a lion, and the second creature like a calf, and the third creature had a face like that of a man, and the fourth creature was like a flying eagle. (Rev. 4:7)*

These four living creatures resemble the most powerful creatures that God created on the surface of the earth—the eagle, the lion, the calf, and man. These angelic creatures, or Seraphim as Isaiah calls them, or living beings as Ezekiel called them, never sleep and are full of eyes. They are a powerful force that God created to serve Him, and I will not guess at why God put them around His throne except to praise Him:

Holy, Holy, Holy, is the Lord God the Almighty, who was and who is and who is to come. (Rev. 4:8b)

Chapter 5

Jesus Steps Before God in Heaven

Chapter 5 is not a hard chapter to read or to understand. There is not a lot of symbolism or mystery here. This chapter can be divided into two main parts. The first seven verses are about Jesus being worthy to receive a prophetic book from God. The other seven verses show us four different groups (creatures, elders, angles, and all other created things) praising God and His Son.

The Book with Seven Seals

And I saw in the right hand of Him who sat on the throne a book written inside and on the back, sealed up with seven seals. (Rev. 5:1)

In this opening verse, we see God on His throne in heaven with a book that is sealed or closed with seven seals. What is this book? This book is like the book of Revelation in that it is about the future of heaven and earth. The visions in this book are mostly about the seven years of tribulation that will come on the earth in the last days.

And one of the elders said to me, "Stop weeping; behold, the Lion that is from the tribe of Judah, the Root of David, has overcome so as to open the book and its seven seals." (Rev. 5:5)

Jesus is called the "Root of David" because He is a direct descendent of David (Matt. 1: 1-16). He is also called a lion because He is the most powerful of the tribe of Judah (Gen. 49: 9).

All in Heaven Give Praise

> *And every created thing which is in heaven and on the earth and under the earth and on the sea, and all things in them, I heard saying, "To Him who sits on the throne, and to the Lamb, be blessing and honor and glory, and dominion forever and ever." (Rev. 5:13)*

In the above verse, it appears that animals go to heaven. I have always wondered about that and other questions about heaven:

1. Do animals go to heaven? Well, in verse 13, it appears that all of God's creatures can go to heaven, and they sing when they get there too! I believe that the animals will talk and sing just as the prophet Balaam's donkey did in Numbers chapter 22. In Revelation 19:14, the saints return to earth on white horses. How did those white horses get to heaven?

   > *Your loving kindness, O Lord, extends to the heavens, your faithfulness reaches to the skies. Your righteousness is like the mountains of God. Your judgments are like a great deep. O Lord, You preserve man and beast. (Ps. 36:5-6)*

2. Do we have harps in heaven? In Revelation 5:8, each elder has one harp; and in Revelation 15:2, the saints that were raptured out of the Great Tribulation are holding the harps of God. I believe that God will give all of us some kind of stringed instrument, and we will know how to play them in that great day.

   > *Great and marvelous are Your works, O Lord God, the Almighty; Righteous and true are Your ways, King of the nations! (Rev. 15:3b)*

3. Are there angels in heaven, and how many? In verse 11, we see myriads of myriads and thousands of thousands of angels. This means ten thousand times ten thousand and thousands and thousands, which means they are innumerable.

And suddenly there appeared with the angel a multitude of the heavenly host praising God and saying, Glory to God in the highest, and on earth peace among men with whom He is pleased. (Lk. 2:13-14)

4. When we die, do we go heaven? Yes, if we are born again in Jesus Christ, our soul will go to heaven when we die. (Matt. 22:29-32; Lk. 23:42-43; Jn. 11:25-26; 2 Cor. 5:8; Heb.12: 22-24; Phil. 1:23)

   And I said to Him, "These are the ones who come out of the great tribulation, and they have washed their robes and made them white in the blood of the Lamb. For this reason, they are before the throne of God; and they serve him day and night in His temple; and He who sits on the throne shall spread His tabernacle over them." (Rev. 7:14-15)

Chapter 6

Six Seals: An Overview of the Tribulation

In the previous chapter, God handed Jesus a sealed book while He was in heaven. This sealed book is filled with visions of future events in heaven and on earth. In this chapter, we will see the Lamb (Jesus) breaking open six of the seven seals. We will see Jesus opening the seventh seal in chapter 8.

> *And I saw when the Lamb broke one of the seven seals, and I heard one of the four living creatures saying as with a voice of thunder, "Come." (Rev. 6:1)*

I believe these seven seals are like a table of contents or a preview of the future events that are going happen all during the seven years of the tribulation. I am convinced, that is why God put the seven seals on the outside of the book, to divide the book into two separate time frames. Sure, the seals were placed there to seal the book; but the dual purpose of these seals has confused readers for centuries.

The First Four Seals

The first four seals that are broken are different-colored horses with riders on them. These riders bring horrible calamities to earth; and they are probably man-made, as opposed to a wrath of God.

1. And I looked, and behold, a white horse, and he who sat on it had a bow; and a crown was given to him, and he went out conquering, and to conquer. (Rev. 6:2)
2. And another, a red horse, went out; and to him who sat on it, it was granted to take peace from the earth, and that men should slay one another; and a great sword was given to him. (Rev. 6:4)
3. And when He broke the third seal, I heard the third creature saying, "Come." And I looked, and behold, a black horse; and he who sat on it had a pair of scales in his hand. (Rev. 6:5)
4. And I looked, and behold, an ashen horse;, and he who sat on it had the name Death; and Hades was following with him. And authority was given to them over a fourth of the earth, to kill with sword and with famine and with pestilence and by the wild beasts of the earth. (Rev. 6:8)

I believe these four seals, or horsemen, could be what Jesus called the "birth pangs" in Matthew 24:8 and Mark 13:8. Look at the chart below and compare John's vision in Revelation 6 with what Jesus said about the last days.

	The Four Horsemen of the Apocalypse	
	Vision	Event
1	White Horse	False Christ
	Rev. 6:2	Matt. 24:5
2	Red Horse	Wars
	Rev. 6:4	Matt. 24:6
3	Black Horse	Famines
	Rev. 6:5	Matt. 24:7
4	Pale Horse	Death
	Rev. 6:8	Matt. 24:9

1. Today, there are many false Christs or religions in the world.
2. This century has never really known peace, and it looks like the next century will have atomic wars.
3. This century has seen the worst famines in human history; and with the world's population still exploding, we could see far worse famines as the world's natural resources are used up or are destroyed.

4. Death and pestilence could be our lot for the twenty-first century as new drug-resistant diseases keep springing up. Also, atomic fallout and biological warfare will cause hundreds of millions of people to suffer in future wars. I believe these four seals could start shortly, but many believe they have already begun. These four horsemen's seals could take us up sometime in the middle of the tribulation. Most of mankind will be ready for one world ruler to help restore peace and order after millions upon millions of the earth's population are killed during the ride of these four horsemen.

The four horsemen that John saw in this vision are like the ones found in Zechariah chapters 1 and 6, and they destroy like the horses in Joel 2:4-10.

> *With the first chariot were red horses, with the second chariot black horses, with the third chariot white horses, and with the fourth chariot strong dappled horses. Then I spoke and said to the angel who was speaking with me, "What are these, my lord?" The angel replied to me, "These are the four spirits of heaven, going forth after standing before the Lord of all the earth . . . to patrol the earth." (Zech. 6:2-7)*

The Fifth Seal Is Broken

> *And when He broke the fifth seal, I saw underneath the alter the souls of those who had been slain because of the word of God, and because of the testimony which they had maintained; and they cried out with a loud voice saying, "How long, O Lord, holy and true, wilt Thou refrain from judging and avenging our blood on those who dwell on the earth?" And there was given to each of them a white robe; and they were told that they should rest for a little while longer, until the number of their fellow servants and brethren who were to be killed even as they had been, should be completed also. (Rev. 6:9-11)*

The fifth seal shows us a vision of Christians in heaven that were killed during the tribulation. Later, Revelation 7:13-14 says these Christians were also killed during the Great Tribulation, when the Antichrist rules the earth in the second half of the tribulation. This fifth seal is very important because it shows that Christians will be on the earth during the greater part of the tribulation. Paul the apostle points out that the rapture of the church will happen during the tribulation and not before the seven years:

> *With regard to the coming of our Lord Jesus Christ and our gathering together to Him, that you not be quickly shaken from your composure or be disturbed either by a spirit or a message or a letter as if from us, to the effect that the day of the Lord has come. Let no one in any way deceive you, for it will not come unless the apostasy comes first, and the man of lawlessness is revealed, the son of destruction. (2 Thess. 2:1b-3)*

Paul is very clear in telling us that we must see these two major signs: the falling away of the faith (apostasy) and the Antichrist showing himself.

The Sixth Seal Is Broken

> *And I looked when He broke the sixth seal, and there was a great earthquake; and the sun became black as sackcloth made of hair, and the whole moon became like blood; and the stars of the sky fell to the earth, as a fig tree casts its unripe figs when shaken by a great wind. And the sky was split apart like a scroll when it is rolled up; and every mountain and island was moved out of their places. (Rev. 6:12-14)*

I believe the sixth seal is a preview of the very end of the Great Tribulation and of the end of the earth! Compare these verses (Rev. 6:12-17) of "John's Visions" with other "End-time Visions" in the Bible. In the chart below, you will see that by comparing the sixth seal with other last-day visions, the sixth seal is giving us a view of the end of the tribulation, not the first half of the tribulation as some teachers would have you believe.

	The Wraths in the Sixth Seal	
	John's Visions	End-Time Visions
1	Great Earthquake	Rev. 16:18
2	Sun Blackened	Joel 2:10
3	Moon Red (changed)	Joel 2:31
4	Stars Fall	Matt. 24:32
5	As Figs	Isa. 13:10
6	Sky Was Split	Isa. 34:2-4
7	Mountain and Islands	Rev. 16:20
8	Men Hide in Caves	Isa. 2:19

If these wraths happened at the start of the tribulation, as many Bible teachers teach, most of mankind would be dead.

> *For the great day of their wrath has come; and who is able to stand? (Rev. 6:17)*

The Seventh Seal Is Broken

> *And when He broke the seventh seal, there was silence in heaven for about half an hour. (Rev. 8:1)*

Chapter 7

The 144,000 and the Tribulation Saints

This chapter is divided into two main subjects—the 144,000 Jewish bond-servants on earth and the great multitude of Christians in heaven. Chapter 7 breaks in between the sixth and the seventh seals. John sees these two groups of saints while in the spirit, possibly to offer a ray of hope to believers on the earth before the tribulation trumpet plagues begin.

The 144,000 Male Jews

> *And I saw another angel ascending from the rising of the sun, having the seal of the living God; and he cried out with a loud voice to the four angels to whom it was granted to harm the earth and sea, saying, "Do not harm the earth or the sea or the trees, until we have sealed the bond-servants of our God on their foreheads." And I heard the number of those who were sealed, one hundred and forty-four thousand sealed from every tribe of the sons of Israel. (Rev. 7:2-4)*

In the first promise above, God shows us that He is a merciful God. He will not allow the earth, sea, and trees to be harmed until His chosen Jews are sealed. They will be protected by a seal on their foreheads, like the Jews whom God showed mercy in Ezekiel 9, when God's wrath was poured out on all unsealed and sinful Jews in Jerusalem. I believe these bond-servants of God will be in the nation of Israel in the last days, and that they will be protected from harm so they can help their brothers.

> And the Lord said to him, "Go through the midst of the city, even through the midst of Jerusalem, and put a mark on the foreheads of the men who sigh and groan over all the abominations which are committed in its midst." But to the others He said in my hearing, "Go through the city after him and strike; do not let your eye have pity, and do not spare." (Ezek. 9:4-5)

In Revelation 14, these 144,000 male Jews are suddenly found in heaven as the first fruits to God and the Lamb, which would mean they are the first raptured or taken up to heaven after the Antichrist appears.

The Tribulation Saints in Heaven

> After these things I looked, and behold a great multitude, which no one could count, from every nation and all tribes and peoples and tongues, standing before the throne and before the Lamb, clothed in white robes, and palm branches were in their hands. (Rev. 7:9)

The second promise in this chapter shows that Christians all over the earth will go directly to heaven when they are killed for their faith during the Great Tribulation.

> And one of the elders answered, saying to me, "These who are clothed in the white robes, who are they, and from where have they come?" And I said to him, "These are the ones who come out of the great tribulation, and they have washed their robes and made them white in the blood of the Lamb." (Rev. 7:13-14)

These great multitudes in white robes are Christian martyrs (Rev. 6:9) that come out of the tribulation because the Antichrist kills them. They do not get raptured out of the earth before the seven-year tribulation begins because we can see these saints, who died for their faith, in Revelation chapters 7 and 8. These elect, or chosen ones, are from all nations and are the saints spoken of in Daniel 7:21 and 11:33; Matthew 24:9; and Revelation 12:17 and 13:7.

> *You too be patient; strengthen your hearts, for the coming of the Lord is near. Do not complain, brethren, against one another, so that you yourselves may not be judged; behold, the Judge is standing right at the door. As an example, brethren, of suffering and patience, take the prophets who spoke in the name of the Lord. We count those blessed who endured. You have heard of the endurance of Job and have seen the outcome of the Lord's dealings, that the Lord is full of compassion and is merciful. (James. 5:8-11)*

Many Christians reading this book have a false hope, believing they will not be here during the tribulation. There hasn't been a single scripture up to this point in the book of Revelation to show that we have been raptured. You cannot find the word "church" after chapters 2 and 3 because John was speaking to the seven churches at his time in the first century (Rev. 1:19b). The apostle Peter has some special words of encouragement for us:

> *Beloved, do not be surprised at the fiery ordeal among you, which comes upon you for your testing, as though some strange thing were happening to you; but to the degree that you share the sufferings of Christ, keep on rejoicing, so that also at the revelation of His glory you may rejoice with exultation. (1 Pet. 4:12-13)*

PART 4

THE FIRST HALF OF THE TRIBULATION

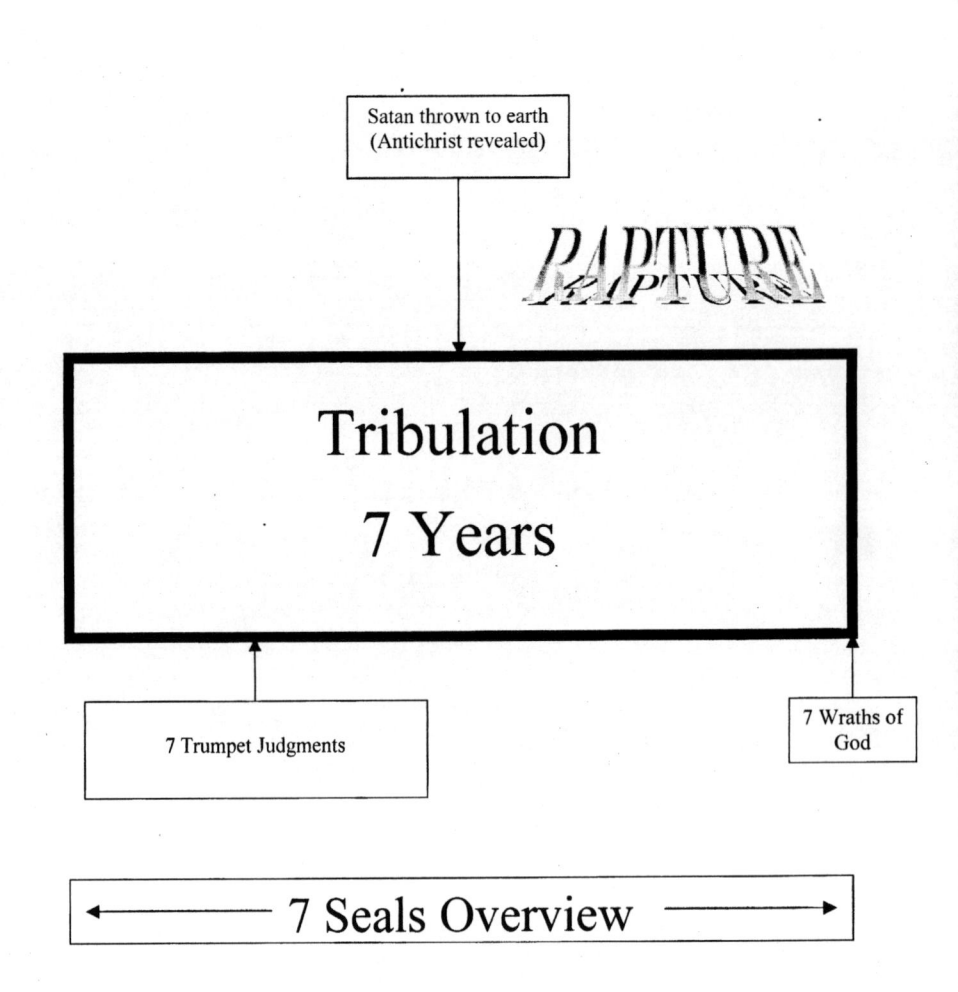

```
            Satan thrown to earth
             (Antichrist revealed)
                      |
                      |        RAPTURE
                      v
┌─────────────────────────────────────────────┐
│                                             │
│               Tribulation                   │
│                 7 Years                     │
│                                             │
└─────────────────────────────────────────────┘
          ^                            ^
          |                            |
  ┌───────────────┐             ┌──────────┐
  │ 7 Trumpet Judgments │       │ 7 Wraths of │
  └───────────────┘             │    God     │
                                └──────────┘

┌─────────────────────────────────────────────┐
│  <─────── 7 Seals Overview ───────>         │
└─────────────────────────────────────────────┘
```

Chapter 8

The Tribulation Begins

When the seventh seal is broken, we see that the book in Jesus's hand can now be opened. To announce this final time, seven trumpets are blown in heaven that will not be heard here on the earth; but their effects will be visible to those who follow prophecy as signs. It will be a time like never been seen on the earth! Four of the seven trumpets are sounded in this chapter. The seven trumpets together will destroy up to one-third of mankind and the earth! In the book of Joshua, we see the priests of Israel blowing seven horns a total of thirteen times before the walls of Jericho fall. Here we see the seven trumpets of God blown before the earth can be destroyed.

> *If a trumpet is blown in a city will not the people tremble . . . Surely the Lord God does nothing unless He reveals His secret counsel to His servants the prophets. (Amos 3:6-7)*

The Seven Trumpet Plagues

- Trumpet 1—one-third of the trees and grass are destroyed (Rev. 8:7)
- Trumpet 2—one-third of the seas are destroyed (Rev. 8:8)
- Trumpet 3—one-third of the fresh water is destroyed (Rev. 8:10)
- Trumpet 4—one-third of the sky is darkened (Rev. 8:12)
- Trumpet 5—five months of torment on mankind (Rev. 9:1-10)
- Trumpet 6—one-third of mankind is killed (Rev. 9:13-21)
- Trumpet 7—Satan is thrown to earth (Rev. 11:15; 12:7-12)

The First Four Trumpets in Chapter 8

> *And the seven angels who had the seven trumpets prepared themselves to sound them. And the first sounded, and there came hail and fire, mixed with blood, and they were thrown to the earth; and a third of the earth was burned up, and all the grass was burned up. (Rev. 8:6-7)*

The four trumpet blasts in Revelation 8 start the calamity on earth that is called the tribulation. Whether these are man-made disasters or judgments from God, it is not clear at all. There are a number of things that could happen today to cause such a worldwide disaster:

1. A giant asteroid crashing to earth
2. A nuclear accident causing a chain reaction
3. The two prophets of God in Revelation 11:6 smiting the earth
4. A world war to unite the earth under one world leader
5. A great earthquake that causes a financial meltdown.

I believe there will be a combination of some of the events above that will usher in the tribulation. This will unite the world's nations and religions under one world leader. Many of the world's religions now are looking for a world leader to eliminate their poverty and starvation. Many of the world's religions mention in their holy writings that a holy man that unites the earth in peace and performs some miracles will be their Messiah!

> *And the fourth angel sounded, and a third of the sun and a third of the moon and a third of the stars were smitten, so that a third of them might be darkened and the day might not shine for a third of it, and the night in the same way. (Rev. 8:12)*

When we have wars and atomic weapons going off in the future, the fourth trumpet will announce in heaven that the earth's skies have lost one-third of their light from the smoke of the fires from the blasts. We will not hear this fourth trumpet blast as we will not hear the other trumpets, but we will see the effects here on earth after they have sounded. I feel that some parts of the world will be spared from some of these disasters. An example would be Israel and Babylon the Great, because they will be destroyed or used later in the tribulation.

> *Thus says the Lord, "Do not learn the ways of the nations, and do not be terrified by the signs of the heavens although the nations are terrified by them." (Jer. 10: 2)*

Chapter 9

Woe, Woe, Woe: More Trumpets

In this chapter, we continue with two more of the seven trumpet plagues that take place in the first half of the tribulation. I believe that they are called the "woes" because they are caused by Satan and his demons, and they affect just about all of mankind. Woe to us!

> *Woe, woe, woe, to those who dwell on the earth, because of the remaining blasts of the trumpet of the three angels who are about to sound! (Rev. 8:13)*

Trumpet 5: Locusts from the Bottomless Pit

> *And the fifth angel sounded, and I saw a star from heaven which had fallen to the earth; and the key of the bottomless pit was given to him. And he opened the bottomless pit; and smoke went up out of the pit, like the smoke of a great furnace; and the sun and the air were darkened by the smoke of the pit. And out of the smoke came forth locusts upon the earth; and power was given them, as the scorpions of the earth have power. And they are told that they should not hurt the grass of the earth, nor any green thing, nor any tree, but only the men who do not have the seal of God on their foreheads. (Rev. 9:1-4)*

What could this plague possibly be that torments man for five months? I have read that some Bible commentators believe it is the locusts from Moses's day attacking people, and some believe the locusts are actually helicopters attacking people in the last days. The Jehovah's Witnesses believe that they are the fifth-plague locusts stinging Christians on earth now, and today that would make their leader the fallen star (probably Satan) that fell from heaven in Revelation 9:1 and 11.

> They have as a king over them, the angel of the abyss; his name in Hebrew is Abaddon, and in the Greek he has the name Apollyon [Destroyer] (Rev. 9:11)

If I had to guess what this fifth trumpet plague is going to be, I would guess that it is an atomic war inspired by the destroyer that causes five months of radioactive contamination over the whole earth. During the five months of contamination, everyone on the earth could get sores or boils like Job, making people wish they were dead. The 144,000 sealed bond-servants of God will be spared from this worldwide, demonic pandemic because they have been chosen for a special work of God.

> They were told not to hurt the grass of the earth, nor any green thing, nor any tree, but only the men who do not have the seal of God on their foreheads. (Rev. 9:4)

Trumpet 6: Army Kills a Third of the Earth

> And the sixth angel sounded, and I heard a voice from the four horns of the golden alter which is before God, one saying to the sixth angel who had the trumpet, "Release the four angels who are bound at the great river Euphrates." And the four angles, who had been prepared for the hour and day and month and year, were released, so that they might kill a third of mankind. And the number of the armies of the horseman was two hundred million; I heard the number of them. (Rev. 9:13-16)

Woe, woe, woe to the earth because a third of mankind is killed with this sixth plague! What kills all these people? Is it an army of two hundred million that comes out of the Middle East inspired by four angles from the abyss? These last three trumpets are demonic in nature, and that is why they are called woes. When the sixth trumpet is sounded just before the middle of the tribulation, could four of the Arab nations that follow Allah be deceived by the four angles from the abyss and become a united army of two hundred million? With this army and the ability to deliver atomic weapons, I believe that Islamic army could start a holy war (jihad) to reclaim Jerusalem and to try to make the whole world convert to Islam. A war like this could destroy a third of the world's population, especially if they attack India whom they hate. The prophet Daniel talked about a beast before the Antichrist's kingdom that looked like a leopard with four heads and four wings. Could four Islamic nations like Iran, Iraq, Pakistan, and Syria become one united Shiite nation like the prophecy of the leopard in Daniel below?

> *After this I kept looking, and behold, another one, like a Leopard, which had on its back four wings of a bird; the beast also had four heads, and dominion was given to it. After this I kept looking in the night visions, and behold a fourth beast, dreadful and terrifying, and extremely strong; and it had large iron teeth. It devoured and crushed and trampled down the remainder with its feet; and it was different from all the beasts that were before it, and it had ten horns. While I was contemplating the horns, behold, another horn, a little one, came up among them, and three of the first horns were pulled out by the roots before it; and behold, this horn possessed eyes like the eyes of a man and a mouth uttering great boasts. (Dan. 7:6-8)*

> *And the beast which I saw was like a leopard, and his feet were like those of a bear, and his mouth like the mouth of a lion. And the dragon gave him his power and his throne and great authority. (Rev. 13:2)*

This leopard of a beast with four heads (maybe four Shiite nations united) might be the six trumpet plague that destroys 1/3 of the world's population (Dan. 7:8-24). If the Antichrist destroys this leopard army and becomes their leader, it will control much of the world's oil supply. With his supernatural powers, the rest of the world would follow him blindly except for the United States and Israel. These countries would need to be destroyed by the Antichrist so that he can boast that he is the greatest world leader ever and that he should be worshiped as a God.

> *But when you see Jerusalem surrounded by armies, then recognize that her desolation is at hand. (Luke 21:20)*

Chapter 10

The Seven Thunders

Chapter 10 is a parenthetical chapter in that we stop in between the sixth and seventh trumpet plagues, breaking the trumpets sequence to hear the seven peals of thunder from God.

> *And he cried out with a loud voice, as when a lion roars; and when he had cried out, the seven peals of thunder utter their voices. When the seven peals of thunder had spoken, I was about to write, and I heard a voice from heaven saying, "Seal up the things which the seven peals of thunder have spoken and do not write them." (Rev. 10:3-4)*

We are not told what these seven peals of thunder are, so I will not comment on them as well as most of the rest of chapter 10.

> *And they said to me, "You must prophesy again concerning many peoples and nations and tongues and kings." (Rev. 10:11)*

Here John is told to keep on prophesying so that he will write the last half of the book of Revelation. Some Bible scholars believe Revelation was written for just the Jews, but verse 11 proves them wrong.

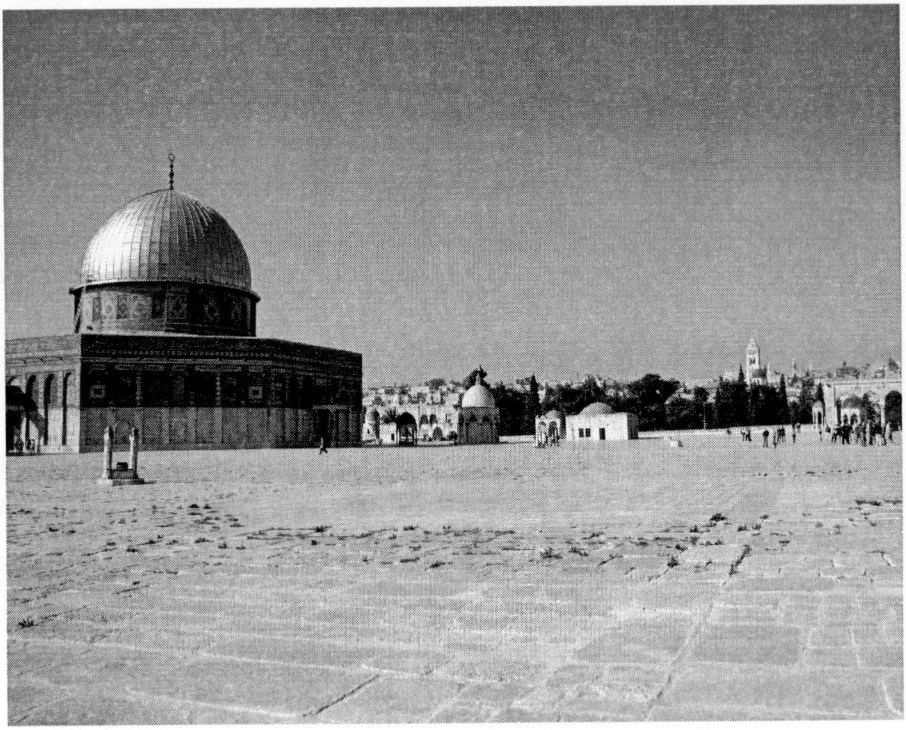

Chapter 11

The Seventh Trumpet

Revelation 11 is divided into three sections. The first part is about the future temple of God in Israel; the second part is about the two witnesses who come to warn the people of Israel that the end is near; and the third part is about the seventh angel of God sounding the last trumpet, which is also called the third woe.

The Temple Rebuilt

> *And there was given me a measuring rod like a staff; and someone said, "Rise and measure the temple of God, and the alter, and those who worship in it. Leave out the court which is outside the temple, and do not measure it, for it has been given to the nations; and they will tread under foot the holy city for forty-two months." (Rev. 11:1-2)*

In verses 1 and 2, John is given a measuring rod to measure the temple of God. Many scholars today say this verse shows that the temple of God is to be rebuilt in the last days so that the Antichrist can take his stand in the temple to deceive the world. This is when the Antichrist will declare himself to be God, and he is called the Abomination of Desolation in Matthew 24:15. The temple of God has not been rebuilt yet, but there is land available just to the north of the Dome of the Rock. This is where Israeli temple groups have drawn up plans to rebuild the temple. Religious

Jews in Israel are presently training priests to begin the sacrifices for the atonement of sins and have a herd of red heifers ready to atone for the sins of these future temple priests.

The Two Witnesses

> *And I will grant authority to my two witnesses, and they will prophesy for twelve hundred and sixty days, clothed in sackcloth. (Rev. 11:3)*

In verses 3-12, we find the two witnesses who prophesy for three and one-half years before the beast kills them. Who are these two witnesses that are spoken of in Revelation? The Bible says that one of them is Elijah the prophet, but it does not say who the other prophet is going to be. Many people feel that the other prophet will be Moses because of the miracles he did. Others feel it will be Enoch because he and Elijah did not die. Some feel it could be John the Baptist because Jesus referred to him as Elijah, and some feel that it could be Zerubbabel because he rebuilt the first temple in Jerusalem and is called one of the olive trees and one of the lamp stands of God (Zech. 4:9-14). Whoever this second prophet is, we will be warned by him and Elijah that we need to repent because the seventh trumpet is about to be sounded, which is when Satan will rule the earth for three and a half years.

> *These are the two olive trees and the two lampstands that stand before the Lord of the earth. (Rev. 11:4)*

Why do we have these two witnesses? They will be there to help turn the people of Israel back to God in the last days. This is why many people in Jesus's day thought that both John the Baptist and Jesus were Elijah the prophet, who is supposed to come back in the last days.

> *Behold, I am going to send you Elijah the prophet before the coming of the great and terrible day of the Lord. And he will restore the hearts of the fathers to their children, and the hearts of the children to their fathers, lest I come and smite the land with a curse. (Mal. 4:5-6)*

When the two witnesses, or prophets, finish their testimony to the Jews in Israel during the first half of the tribulation (and maybe help rebuild the third temple), the beast (Antichrist) is going to kill them.

When they have finished their testimony, the beast that comes up out of the abyss will make war with them, and overcome them and kill them. (Rev. 11:7)

The Seventh Trumpet

The second woe is past; behold, the third woe is coming quickly. And the seventh angel sounded; and there arose loud voices in heaven, saying, "The kingdom of the world has become the kingdom of our Lord, and of His Christ; and He will reign forever and ever." (Rev. 11:14-15)

With the sounding of the seventh trumpet, Christ finishes taking His reign with God in heaven (Rev. 11:17). With the sounding of the seventh trumpet, the first thing that Jesus does is to have Satan thrown out of heaven. This is the third woe that we were warned about (Rev. 12:7-12). Many Christians believe that Satan is either in hell or on the earth only and could never be in heaven. But one would only need to look at the book of Job chapters 1 and 2 or Zechariah 3:1 to see that Satan is allowed in heaven.

And the nations were enraged, and Thy wrath came, and the time came for the dead to be judged, and the time to give their reward to Thy bond-servants the prophets and to the saints and to those who fear Thy name, the small and the great, and to destroy those who destroy the earth. (Rev. 11:18)

This verse could be a prophetic announcement in heaven by the twenty-four elders of the things that will happen at the end of the tribulation.

And the temple of God which is in heaven was opened; and the ark of His covenant appeared in His temple. (Rev. 11:19a)

I believe that the Old Testament Ark of the Covenant, built by Moses, will be found in the last days and placed in the third temple. If it is found under the temple mount in Jerusalem, as many Jews believe it will be, or being kept in Ethiopia until the last days, it remains to be seen. In verse 19a, the ark is taken to heaven by God in order to keep it out of the hands of the Antichrist.

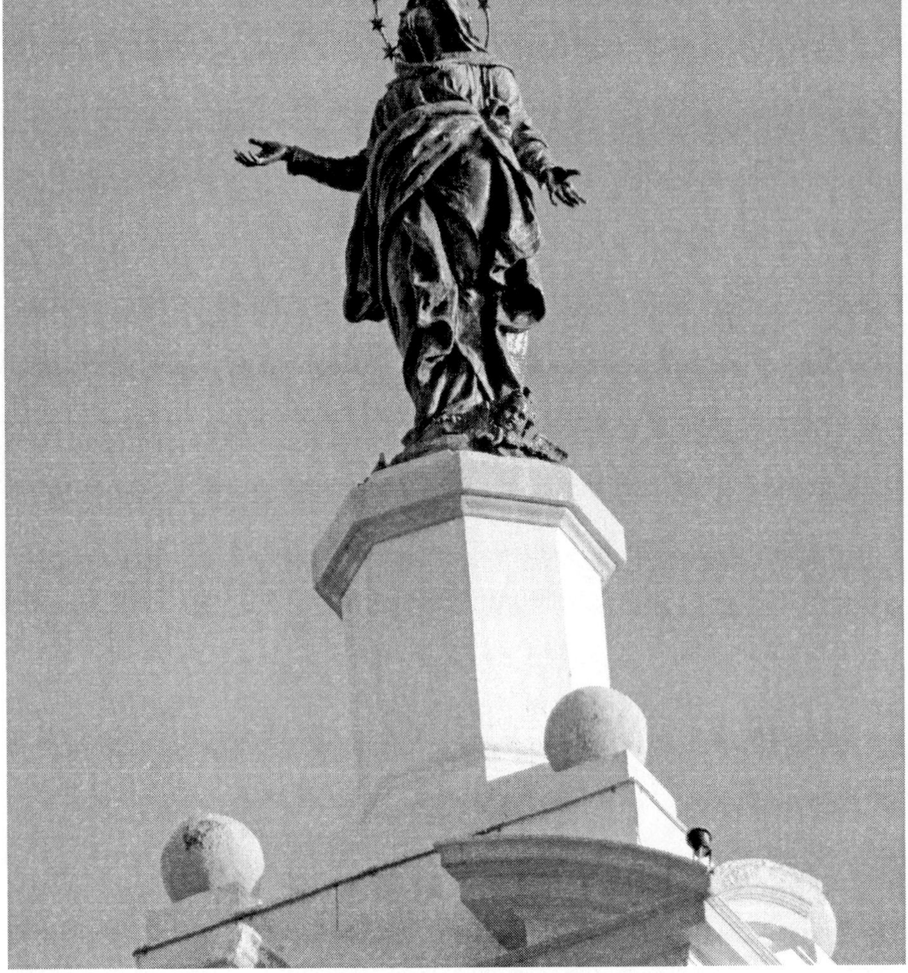

Chapter 12

Satan the Destroyer Comes to Earth

Revelation 12 takes us to the midpoint of the tribulation, and the main subject of this chapter is Satan and his major evil acts all through time. In this chapter, Satan will go after Jesus, cause war in heaven twice, try to destroy the nation of Israel in the last days, and kill all Christians for three and a half years. Satan is called in four different names in this chapter:

1. Great Red Dragon (Rev. 12:3)
2. Devil (Rev. 12:9)
3. Satan (Rev. 12:9)
4. Serpent of Old (Rev. 12:9)

The Woman

> *And a great sign appeared in heaven; a woman clothed with the sun, and the moon under her feet, and on her head a crown of twelve stars; and she was with child; and she cried out, being in labor and in pain to give birth. (Rev. 12:1-2)*

In verses 1 and 2, John sees a great sign in heaven. This sign is a vision from the past when Mary, who was a Jew, gave birth to Jesus. The crown of twelve stars on Mary's head is to show that she symbolizes Israel and the twelve tribes. In Genesis 37:9-10, Joseph has a vision with eleven stars bowing down to him. The stars represent the tribes of Israel as they do in this sign.

> *And she gave birth to a son, a male child, who is to rule all nations with a rod of iron; and her child was caught up to God and to His throne. And the woman fled into the wilderness where she had a place prepared by God, so that she might be nourished for one thousand two hundred and sixty days. (Rev. 12:5-6)*

In verse 5, she gives birth to a male child, Jesus, who will rule the nations with an iron rod for one thousand years, beginning in Revelation 19:15. In verse 6, we are taken into the future when the woman, who represents Israel in the last days, flees into the wilderness for three and a half years to escape the Antichrist. In the Gospel of Matthew, Jesus tells Israel (the woman) to flee when they see Satan in the temple:

> *Therefore when you see the ABOMINATION OF DESOLATION which was spoken of through Daniel the prophet, standing in the holy place (let the reader understand), then let those who are in Judea flee to the mountains; let him who is on the house top not go down to get the things out that are in the house; and let him who is in the field not turn back to get his cloak. (Matt. 24:15-18)*

In the time of Moses, Israel survived in the wilderness for forty years. Today, this wilderness is located in Saudi Arabia and Jordan, which was called the Land of Midian (Exodus 2:15), and the regions of Edom, Moab, and Ammon (Dan. 11:41, Isa. 16:14). So when she (Israel) flees into the wilderness, this time for three and a half years, it should be easier because they might have the 144,000 bond-servants of God leading them as deliverers (Obad. 1:21).

Daniel the prophet said that Satan would enter into Israel but would not enter the land where Israel was wandering.

> *He will also enter the Beautiful Land, and many countries will fall; but these will be rescued out of his hand: Edom, Moab and the foremost of the sons of Ammon. (Dan. 11:41)*

> *Therefore, behold I will allure her, bring her into the wilderness, and speak kindly to her. Then I will give her her vineyards from there, and the valley of Achor as a door of hope. And she will sing there as in the days of her youth, and when she came up from the land of Egypt. (Hos. 2: 14, 15)*

> *Alas! For that day is great, there is none like it; and it is the time of Jacob's distress, but he will be saved from it. (Jer. 30:7)*

These wildernesses are mostly to the southeast of Israel and are very rugged. Maybe God will speak to them from the real Mount Sinai (Jabal al-Lawz) in Saudi Arabia during the three and a half years of the Great Tribulation.

> *And I shall bring you out from the peoples and gather you from the lands where you are scattered, with a mighty hand and with an outstretched arm and with wrath poured out; and I shall bring you into the wilderness of the peoples, and there I shall enter into judgment with you face to face. "As I entered into judgment with your fathers in the wilderness of the land of Egypt, so I will enter into judgment with you," declares the Lord God. (Ezek. 20:34, 36)*

Satan Comes to Earth

> *And another sign appeared in heaven: and behold, a great red dragon having seven heads and ten horns, and on his heads were seven diadems. And his tail swept away a third of the stars of heaven, and threw them to the earth. And the dragon stood before the woman who was about to give birth, so that when she gave birth he might devour her child. (Rev. 12:3-4)*

In the above verses, Satan comes to earth to do his dirty work. In the future, he will come back as the dragon with seven heads and ten horns. The heads are symbolic of seven great kingdoms in history, and the horns are symbolic of ten future world leaders that he will have under his power, as seen in Revelation 17:12-13. In Jesus's day, Satan tried to destroy Him three times—as a child in Bethlehem, after He had spent forty days in the wilderness, and by entering Judas. Also in this verse, we can see where Satan caused one-third of the angels to be thrown to earth from heaven. At the midpoint of the tribulation, the angels and Satan, who are in heaven for a war, are thrown out of heaven forever by the archangel Michael, as seen below:

> *And there was war in heaven, Michael and his angels waging war with the dragon. And the dragon and his angels waged war. (Rev. 12:7)*
> *And the great dragon was thrown down, the serpent of old who is called the devil and Satan, who deceives the whole world: he was thrown down to the earth, and his angels were thrown down with him. (Rev. 12:9)*

> *For this reason, rejoice, O heavens and you who dwell in them. Woe to the earth and the sea, because the devil has come down to you, having great wrath, knowing that he has only a short time. (Rev. 12:12)*

In verses 7 through 12, after the seventh trumpet is blown, there is a war in heaven. In this war, Michael and his angels defeat Satan and his angels. After losing the war, Satan (and his angels) is thrown to earth. He is very mad, having great wrath. This is called a woe, which is the third woe at the seventh trumpet (Rev. 8:13, 11:14, 12:12). This seventh trumpet (Satan) is our visible sign that the last trumpet plague is sounding. It might help to explain the following scripture with regards to the rapture and its timing:

> *Behold, I tell you a mystery; we will not all sleep, but we will all be changed, in a moment, in the twinkling of an eye, at the last trumpet. (1 Cor. 15:51-52)*

The Woman and Her Children Flee

> *And the two wings of the great eagle were given to the woman, in order that she might fly into the wilderness to her place, where she was nourished for a time and times and half a time, from the presence of the serpent. (Rev. 12:14)*

To understand this vision of a woman with eagle's wings, one would only have to look at Moses and the Israelites in the book of Exodus when God gave them His protection when they were in the wilderness for forty years.

> *And Moses went up to God, and the Lord called to him from the mountain, saying, "Thus you shall say to the house of Jacob and tell the sons of Israel: 'You yourselves have seen what I did to the Egyptians, and how I bore you on eagles wings, and brought you to Myself.'" (Ex. 19:3-4)*

Satan is going to send a flood of armies against Israel in the last days, and most Jews will fight rather than flee into the wilderness. I believe that God is going to spare one-third of the Jews who fled (Zech. 13:8-9).

> *And the serpent poured water like a river out of his mouth after the woman, so that he might cause her to be swept away with the flood. And the earth helped the woman and the earth opened its month and drank up the river which the dragon poured out of his mouth. (Rev. 12:15-16)*

When Satan sees that many of the Jews in Israel have fled into the wilderness and are protected by God, he will go after the Christians of the earth because the rapture of the church has not happened yet.

> *And the dragon was enraged with the woman, and went off to make war with the rest of her offspring, who keep the commandments of God and hold to the testimony of Jesus. (Rev. 12:17)*

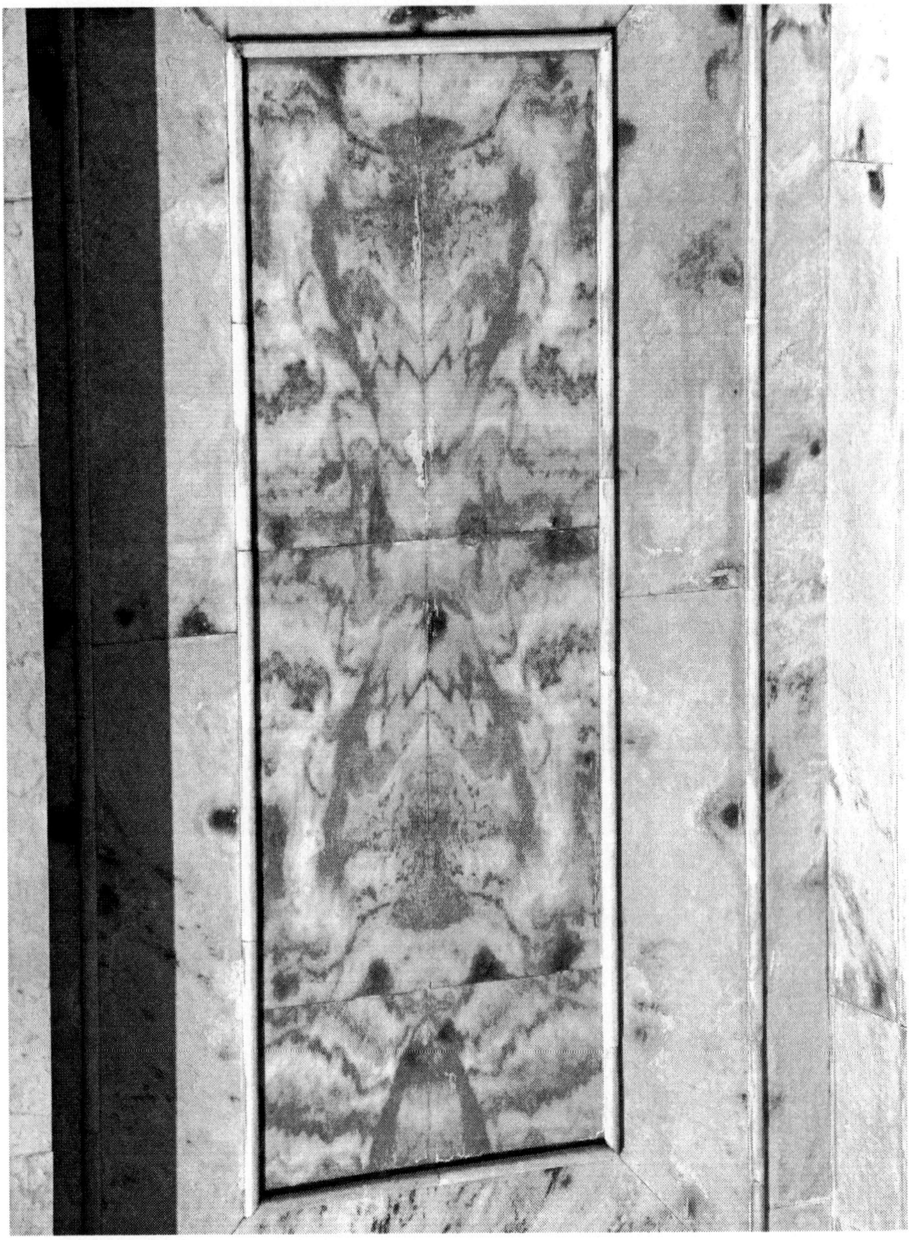

PART 5

THE SECOND HALF OF THE TRIBULATION

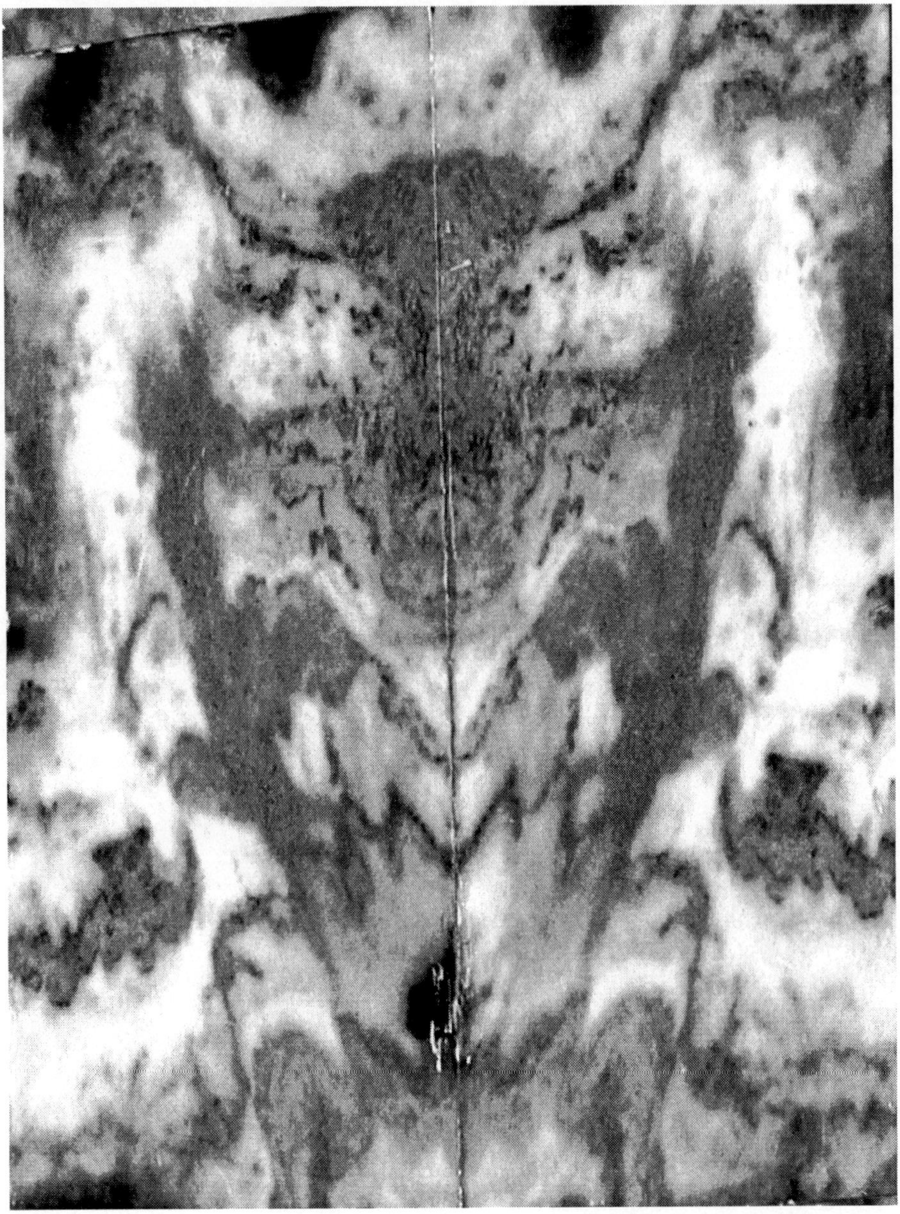

Chapter 13

The Beast and the False Prophet (666)

Chapter 13 is the midpoint of the tribulation. It is about two very evil people that control the earth during the Great Tribulation, which is the last three and a half years of the tribulation. In chapter 12, we saw how Satan came to earth throughout history to deceive and destroy God's people. In this chapter, we will see an *unholy trinity* take place when Satan gives power to the two beasts. One is going to be the future world ruler known as the Antichrist, and the other will be called "the false prophet." These three will deceive most of the earth, even many of the elect or Christians!

The First Beast (Antichrist)

> *And he stood on the sand of the seashore. And I saw a beast coming up out of the sea, having ten horns and seven heads, and on his ten horns were ten diadems, and on his heads were blasphemous names. (Rev. 13:1)*

In verse 1, we see the beast coming out of the sea having seven heads, ten horns, ten crowns, and blasphemous names on his heads. The word "sea" means that the beast comes from the human race (Rev. 17:15). The "seven heads" represent six past kingdoms of the earth, with the seventh being the kingdom of the beast or Antichrist (Rev. 17:8-11). Below is a list of those kingdoms that the heads may represent:

Seven Beast Heads Representation

Egyptian	±1000 BC
Assyrian	±700 BC
Babylonian	±600 BC
Medo-Persian	±536 BC
Greek	±336 BC
Roman	±100 BC
Ten Leaders (maybe a United Europe)	AD ±2000

The "ten horns" might be ten kings, or ten very rich world leaders that give the beast (the seventh head) his power to become the world ruler. Together, they will wage a war against Jesus when He returns (Rev. 17:14). The "seven blasphemous names" could mean that these world kings considered themselves as gods and had no respect for God during their reign. In the Old Testament, the prophet Daniel showed us more about this beast and some of the ten kings that ruled the world in Daniel 2:28-45 and 7:2-28.

> *And the beast which I saw was like a leopard, and his feet were like those of a bear, and his mouth like the mouth like the mouth of a lion. And the dragon gave him his power and his throne and great authority. (Rev. 13:2)*

This vision of the beast may look and sound weird, but these animals are really symbolic of the beast's strength and evilness, especially toward the saints and Israel, as seen in the book of Hosea:

> *Yet I have been the Lord your God since the land of Egypt; and you were not to know any god except Me, for there is no savior besides Me. I cared for you in the wilderness, in the land of drought. As they had their pasture, they became satisfied, and being satisfied, their heart became proud; therefore they forgot Me. So I will be like a lion to them; like a leopard I will lie in wait by the wayside. I will encounter them like a bear robbed of her cubs, and I will tear open their chests; there I will also devour them like a lioness, as*

> *a wild beast would tear them. It is your destruction, O Israel, that you are against Me, against your help. (Hos. 13:4, 9)*

> *And I saw one of his heads as if it had been slain, and his fatal wound was healed. And the whole earth was amazed and followed after the beast. (Rev. 13:3)*

In verse 3, the beast (future world leader) is killed but, to the amazement of the whole earth, comes back to life. When he is killed, is it possible that Moslem extremists will chop off his head? When the world leader is killed, and he is brought back to life from the abyss (Rev. 17:8a) by Satan, most of the world will believe he is a God. When the Antichrist is raised from the dead, Satan will give him supernatural powers. Satan will also give these powers to the false prophet to make him look like Elijah and act as a messianic forerunner proclaiming the beast as the Messiah. Many religions, including Jews, Arabs, and Christians, will turn to worship him at this time, especially when he is in the third temple in Jerusalem.

The Abomination of Desolation

> *And there was given to him a mouth speaking arrogant words and blasphemies; and authority to act for forty-two months was given to him. (Rev. 13:5)*

Wow, now the world is in for it; and they don't even know it! We have been warned about this evil one by Daniel the prophet (Dan. 11:31) and by Jesus (Matt. 24:15). His blasphemy is the middle of the tribulation; and from this point on, we have the Great Tribulation (Matt. 24:21). It is in Revelation 13:4-6 that we see the beast open his mouth to blaspheme against God in His temple in Jerusalem. When we see this act, Jesus told us it would be "the last generation." I believe this is the key sign to the end of the earth, not the year 1948 when Israel became a nation again.

> *Even so you too, when you see all these things, recognize that He is near, right at the door. Truly I say to you, this generation will not pass away until all these things take place. (Matt. 24:33, 34)*

In 1900, 1914, 1948, 1975, and even in 2000, many people have believed that they were in the last generation; but none of these dates had the key scriptural sign! Jesus said, *"Therefore when you see the ABOMINATION OF DESOLATION . . . standing in the holy place,"* (Matt.24:15) that is the key sign! Paul said about this and added another sign: *"Let no one in any way deceive you, for it will not come unless the apostasy (falling away of Christians) comes first, and the man of lawlessness is revealed, the son of destruction" (2 Thess. 2:3).*

> *And it was given to him to make war with the saints and to overcome them; and authority over every tribe and people and tongue and nation was given him. (Rev. 13:7)*

In verse 7, the beast is granted the authority to make war with the saints and to overcome them. In the Gospels, Jesus warned us to flee if we lived in Judea, just as God warned Lot and his family to flee from Sodom and Gomorrah. But if we live somewhere else, we'll need to pray for the rapture to happen quickly or pray for God to direct us in those last days. Below are some words of wisdom from our Lord about killing and captivity, which goes along with what Jesus taught in Beatitudes (Matt. 5:38, 48):

> *If anyone is destined for captivity, to captivity he goes; if anyone kills with the sword, with the sword he must be killed. Here is the perseverance and the faith of the saints. (Rev. 13:10)*

In Daniel 8:24-25, we are warned that the Antichrist will destroy the holy people while they were at ease. There will be great distress in the land and wrath upon this people (Luke 21:23). The Antichrist will rule the world in the last days, and the people of the earth will worship him and his statue that talks in the last days (Rev. 13:14-15). One Catholic writer says that the Catholic Church is going to make the world ruler the pope in the last days; and since they already pray to statues, could the Antichrist or even the false prophet, be a Catholic? Desmond A. Birch says, "A man who will subsequently be known as a great saint (king) will ultimately be elected pope near the end . . . . The Russians and Prussians will subsequently be totally defeated by the Great King." In Daniel, we can see that the Antichrist might be born a Jew because he shows no regard for the God of his fathers (Dan. 11:37). And if he is a Jew, many believe he will come from the tribe of Dan because that tribe is not mentioned with the other Jewish tribes in the scriptures of the last days. In Genesis 49, Jacob summoned his sons to tell them what would befall them or their tribe later:

> *Dan shall be a serpent in the way, a horned snake in the path, that bites the horse's heels, so that his rider falls backward. (Gen. 49:17)*

Another Beast (The False Prophet)

And I saw another beast coming up out of the earth; and he had two horns like a lamb, and he spoke as a dragon. And he exercises all the authority of the first beast and those who dwell in it to worship the first beast, whose fatal wound was healed. (Rev. 13:11-12)

In verses 11 and 12, we see another beast that appears on the earth. He is called the false prophet in Revelation 19:20. This false prophet will deceive most of the people of the earth. His chief aim is to promote the worship of the first beast. Here are several reasons that I believe he will be able to deceive people:

1. He is a prophet, so he is probably a religious person with a charismatic personality.
2. He performs great miracles.
3. He causes fire to come out of heaven so many will believe he's Elijah.
4. He exercises *all* the authority of the first beast.
5. He has two horns, so he probably has the power of a king and a holy man. So he could be a future national leader that just happens to be a saintly leader as well.
6. He makes an image of the beast speak (computer, statue?).

"666"

And he causes all, the small and the great, and the rich and the poor, and the free men and the slaves, to be given a mark on their right hand, or on their forehead, and he provides that no one should be able to buy or to sell, except the one who has the mark, either the name of the beast or the number of his name. Here is wisdom. Let him who has understanding calculate the number of the beast, for the number is that of a man; and his number is six hundred and sixty-six. (Rev. 13:16, 18)

In verses 16-18, the false prophet causes all people to receive a mark on their right hand or their forehead. If they do not receive it, they will not be able to buy or sell; and they will be killed. What is this mark?

- For years people believed it was just the number 666. You could see it used in many of the movies in the seventies and eighties.

- Most born-again Christians now believe it is a universal product code or bar code that can be found on everything we buy now. If this were used, the beast could keep you from buying or selling anything without using his master ID system.
- There are computer chips so thin and small that they can be inserted in your skin, possibly with a tattooed symbol of the Antichrist. This mark, or tattoo, could be like a swastika with eighteen bar lines in it or a religious symbol like the Star of David with eighteen lines. Tattoos are quite common now, and another tattoo would not mean that much in today's generation. The reason that I have said these marks could possibly contain eighteen lines is to represent the configuration of "666"—six plus six plus six equals eighteen.

If anyone worships the beast and his image, and receives a mark on his forehead or upon his hand he also will drink of the wrath of God, which is mixed in full strength in the cup of His anger; and he will be tormented with fire and brimstone in the presence of the holy angels and in the presence of the Lamb. (Rev. 13:10)

As we see in this verse, the wrath of God still has not happened; but it will be severe on those people who receive the mark and worship his image. The second commandment of God teaches us not to worship or serve images or idols (Deut. 5:8-10). But many churches today do not teach the second commandment anymore! They take the second commandment out of their church books and add another commandment in its place. Or they hide the second commandment somewhere in the first commandment, even though the second commandment is still in their Bibles! This teaching will lead many religious people to worship the Antichrist and his image in the last days.

You shall not make for yourself an idol, of any likeness of what is in heaven above or on the earth beneath or in the water under the earth. You shall not worship them or serve them; for I, the Lord your God, am a jealous God. (Deut. 5:8-9)

Rapture

| The 7th Trumpet | **The Great Tribulation**

3 1/2 Years | Battle of Armageddon |

- Antichrist Revealed
- 7 Wraths of God

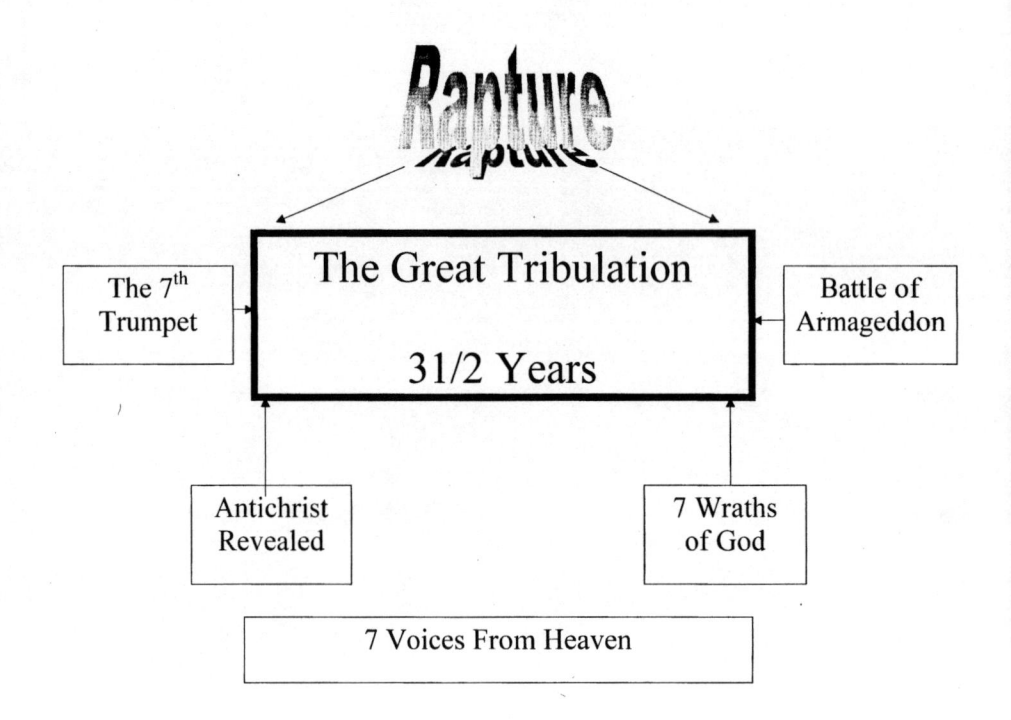

7 Voices From Heaven

Chapter 14

The Seven Voices from Heaven

In chapter 13, we saw how the beast and the false prophet are going to be running the earth during the last three and a half years of the tribulation. Chapter 14 also takes place in the second half of the tribulation; but in this chapter, we will see seven voices from heaven helping mostly believers get through this Great Tribulation. The first voice is the 144,000 bond-servants of God in heaven. Then there are the six other angelic voices from the heavens to announce other judgments or warnings.

The Seven Angelic Announcements:

1. The voices of the 144,000 (vv. 2-3)
2. The Gospel preached to the whole earth (vv. 6-7)
3. Babylon has fallen (v. 8)
4. Worship of the beast warning (vv. 9-11)
5. Encouragement for the saints (vv. 12-13)
6. Harvest of Christians (vv. 14-16)
7. Harvest of non-Christian armies (vv. 17-20)

The 144,000 and Their Angelic Voice

And I looked, and behold, the Lamb was standing on Mount Zion, and with Him one hundred and forty-four thousand, having His name and the name of His Father written on their foreheads. And I heard a voice from heaven. (Rev. 14:1, 2a)

In verse 1, we see the Lamb standing on Mount Zion with the 144,000 rescued or purchased Jews. This Mount Zion is in heaven, though some teachers believe this is taking place on earth in Jerusalem. Here are some reasons why I feel this is in heaven:

1. The Lamb in verse 1 does not return until the end of the tribulation (Rev. 19:11).
2. The four living creatures and the elders are in heaven (Rev. 5:6, 12:16).
3. Revelation 14:3 says that they were *purchased* from the earth.
4. Mount Zion is symbolic of heaven (Heb. 12:22).

And I heard the number of those who were sealed, one hundred and forty-four thousand sealed from every tribe of the sons of Israel. (Rev. 7: 4)

These are the ones who have not been defiled with women, for they have kept themselves chaste. These are the ones who follow the Lamb wherever He goes. These have been purchased from among men as first fruits to God and to the Lamb. (Rev. 14:4)

In Revelation 7:4 we can see that the 144,000 bond-servants are male Jews that have been purchased from the earth as the first fruits to God and the Lamb. A literal interpretation of this verse would mean that these Jews are the first group raptured, or taken from the earth, and that no other rapture could have taken place yet! In 1 Corinthians 15:20, Christ is called the first fruits; so in like manner, these 144,000 saints are the first fruits to be raptured, while the Christians will get to be raptured later in this chapter.

Israel was holy to the Lord, the first of His harvest. (Jer. 2:3a)

In Ezekiel 9, God sends an angel to Jerusalem to put a mark on the foreheads of men who do not practice sin or worship idols. This mark keeps these Jewish men safe over twenty-six hundred years ago, and it will protect the 144,000 during the first part of the tribulation. I believe that they will help many from the Jewish nation who flee into the wilderness of Jordan and Saudi Arabia where God will protect them for three and a half years as He did during the time of Moses. In Isaiah 16:1-4, the fleeing Jews appear to stop and rest at the ancient wilderness city of Sela (Petra) before heading to the mountain of Moses to be kept safe from the destroyer (Satan).

> *From Sela by way of the wilderness to the mountain of the daughter of Zion. Then, like fleeing birds . . . Hide the outcasts . . . be a hiding place to them from the destroyer. (Isa.16:1b, 3b, 4a)*

> *In the thickets of Arabia you must spend the night . . . . Being water for the thirsty . . . Meet the fugitive with bread, for they have fled from the swords. (Isa. 21:13b, 15a)*

The Second Angelic Voice

> *And I saw another angel flying in midheaven, having an eternal gospel to preach to those who live on the earth, and to every nation and tribe and tongue and people; and he said with a loud voice, "Fear God, and give Him glory, because the hour of His judgment has come." (Rev. 14:6-7)*

In verses 6-7, the first angel, or second voice, preaches the Gospel to every nation and tongue on earth from midheaven. This is God's last call for salvation to a world that persists in rejecting Him. How this angel's message is completed is a mystery to me. Some say it will be the 144,000 Jews who will fulfill this announcement, but I cannot find them witnessing anywhere in the Bible. It is possible that the Christians, during that last hour, will be called by the Holy Spirit and this angel to finish spreading the Gospel to the world. Since the hour of His judgment is coming sometime during what is called "The Great Tribulation," Christians will need to remember what Jesus told the church in Philadelphia to keep his word before the hour of testing. We will be raptured before that hour comes at the end of the tribulation.

> *Because you have a little power, and have kept My word, and have not denied my name . . . I also will keep you from the hour of testing . . . I am coming quickly; hold fast what you have, so that no one will take your crown. (Rev. 3:8b, 11)*

The Third Angelic Voice

> *And another angel, a second one, followed, saying, "Fallen, fallen is Babylon the great, she who has made all the nations drink of the wine of the passion of her immorality." (Rev. 14:8)*

In verse 8, the second angel, or third voice, declares that Babylon the Great has fallen. It is my belief that Babylon the Great is destroyed here, as the vision was written. Revelation chapters 17 and 18 explain a lot more about who Babylon the Great is and her destruction by the Antichrist and the other nations that help him.

The Fourth Angelic Voice

> *And another angel, a third one, followed them, saying with a loud voice, "If anyone worships the beast and his image, and receives a mark on his forehead or upon his hand, he also will drink of the wine of the wrath of God." (Rev. 9:10)*

In verses 9-10, the third angel, or fourth voice, warns the people of the earth not to worship the beast or to receive his mark. How this warning is delivered to the earth is unknown, but we are going to be warned. I believe many deceived Christian churches will encourage their congregations to receive the mark (666) on their hand or forehead because they do not follow the word of God. Today, many of these deceived Christian churches allow homosexuality (even in the clergy), the worship of idols, premarital sex, abusive language, adultery, and so forth. The mark might be encouraged as a sign of holiness as it is in Hinduism with the round red mark on the forehead or a cross that looks like the ash cross in Catholicism.

The Fifth Angelic Voice

> *Here is the perseverance of the saints who keep the commandments of God and their faith in Jesus. And I heard a voice from heaven, saying, "Write, Blessed are the dead who die in the Lord from now on!" "Yes," says the Spirit, "that they may rest from their labors, for their deeds follow them." (Rev. 14:12-13)*

This can be a difficult sentence to understand, but I believe it was put here for our encouragement, or perseverance, during our persecution (Rev. 13:10). When true Christians refuse to receive the mark of the beast, the forces of the Antichrist will kill many. God is letting us know that we will be blessed if we die before the rapture happens, because our soul is going straight to heaven to be with God and Jesus (Rev. 7:13-17).

The Sixth Angelic Voice

And I looked, and behold, a white cloud, and sitting on the cloud was one like a son of man, having a golden crown on His head, and a sharp sickle in His hand. And another angel came out of the temple, crying out with a loud voice to Him who sat on the cloud, "Put in your sickle and reap, because the hour to reap has come, because the harvest of the earth is ripe." And He who sat on the cloud swung His sickle over the earth; and the earth was reaped. (Rev. 14:14-16)

THE RAPTURE HAS JUST HAPPENED! In verses 14-16, another angel from heaven cries out to put in a reaper's sickle because the harvest is ripe. I believe that this is where God takes the Christians out of the earth (rapture). Now the wrath of God can fall on the earth, as we will see in the next two chapters of Revelation. All of the Christians who have survived up to this point in the Great Tribulation will have their bodies changed from earthly ones to heavenly ones:

Behold, I tell you a mystery; we shall not all sleep, but we shall all be changed, in a moment, in the twinkling of an eye, at the last trumpet; for the trumpet will sound, and the dead will be raised imperishable, and we shall be changed. (1 Cor. 15:51-52)

The last trumpet is the third woe, which is Satan being thrown down to earth in Revelation 8:13; 11:14, 15a; 12:12. We will not hear this trumpet, but we will see a harvest to heaven as Satan toots his horn of evil works. This harvest will be

- the rapture of the two witnesses;
- the 144,000 male Jews purchased from the earth;
- the Christians raptured to heaven's sea of glass.

But when the crop permits, he immediately puts in the sickle, because the harvest has come. (Mk. 4:29)

Then there shall be two men in the field; one will be taken, and one will be left . . . Two women will be grinding at the mill; one will be taken, and one will be left. (Matt. 24:40, 41)

The Seventh Angelic Voice

And another angel came out of the temple which is in heaven, and he also had a sharp sickle. And another angel, the one who has power over fire, came out from the alter; and he called with a loud voice to him who had the sharp sickle, saying, "Put in your sharp sickle, and gather the clusters from the vine of the earth, because her grapes are ripe." And the angel swung his sickle to the earth, and gathered the clusters from the vine earth, and threw them into the great wine press of the wrath of God. (Rev. 14:17-19)

In verses 18 and 19, the fifth angel, or seventh voice, cried out for the sickle. With it, the armies of the world are gathered in Israel for the battle of Armageddon. They are not carried off to Israel by an angel with this announcement, but their leaders are influenced by demons to start bringing them to the "valley of decision" at Armageddon (Revelation 16:13-14).

*Put in the sickle, for the harvest is ripe. Come, tread, for the wine press is full; the vats overflow, for their wickedness is great. Multitudes, multitudes in the valley of decision! For **the day of the Lord** is near in the valley of decision! (Joel 3: 13-14)*

I have added the bold print in the scriptures above to show that "the wrath of God and the day of the Lord" are at the end of the tribulation. Also see (2 Thess. 2:2-3)

Chapter 15

The Saints Are All in Heaven

Chapter 15 is the shortest chapter in Revelation with only eight verses. It can be considered an introduction to chapter 16, the wrath of God. Chapter 15 is a view of what takes place in heaven near the end of the tribulation. There are no Christians left on the earth because they are in heaven, giving glory to God.

The Saints in Heaven

> *And I saw, as it were, a sea of glass mixed with fire, and those who had come off victorious from the beast and from his image and from the number of his name, standing on the sea of glass, holding harps of God. (Rev. 15:2)*

This verse is a proof that the saints are going to be raptured from the earth before the wrath of God. These saints were victorious because they were not killed or fooled by the Antichrist. They are together with all the saints from throughout history. They are standing on a sea of glass that is mixed with fire. This fire could be a symbol of the Holy Spirit landing on the saints, as at the day of Pentecost (Acts 2:3). They all have harps, or stringed instruments, to make beautiful sounds of praise for His marvelous works. And they sang the song of Moses, the bond-servant of God, and the song of the Lamb, saying,

Great and marvelous are Thy works, O Lord God, the Almighty; Righteous and true are Thy ways, Thou King of the nations. "Who will not fear, O Lord, and glorify Thy name? For Thou alone art holy; For All the Nations will come and worship before Thee, For Thy righteous acts have been revealed." (Rev. 15:3-4)

Read this Song of Moses in Exodus 15:1-18, and you will be blessed. If you are in a group, read it aloud.

Chapter 16

The Wrath of God

And the temple was filled with smoke from the glory of God and from His power; and no one was able to enter the temple until the seven plagues of the seven angels were finished. (Rev. 15:8)

Chapter 16 brings us to the destruction of the earth and the end of this age as God goes into His temple by Himself until the tribulation is over. The Christians are no longer found on earth because they are reaped, or raptured, (Rev. 14:16) out to the sea of glass in heaven. Hallelujah! Below are listed the wraths that befall men at the end of the earth. They are going to take place as they are written and are not symbolic of things now or in the past. As in the days of Noah (Gen. 7) and Moses (Ex. 7), these events are really going to happen!

The Seven Bowls of Wrath

1. A wicked sore came upon those who receive the mark (v. 2).
2. The sea (ocean) became as blood (v. 3).
3. The rivers of water became blood (v. 4).
4. The sun burnt men with great heat (vv. 8-9).
5. The beast's kingdom is darkened (v. 10).
6. The Euphrates River was dried up for the kings of the east (v. 12).
7. And every island and mountain is no longer found (v. 20).

> *And I heard a loud voice from the temple, saying to the seven angels, "Go and pour out the seven bowls of the wrath of God into the earth." (Rev. 16:1)*

The First Angel's Bowl

> *And the first angel went and poured out his bowl into the earth; and it became a loathsome and malignant sore upon the men who had the mark of the beast and who worshiped his image. (Rev. 16:2)*

In the last days, man will not be able to buy or sell unless he has a mark on his right hand or his forehead (Rev. 13:16-17). This mark could be a sign of allegiance to the beast and a promise to protect them in times of trouble. He will probably have a tattooed bar code for each person or some kind of computer chip in it too. This tattoo might be in the shape of a cross if the Antichrist is someone like the pope. In the Catholic book *The Bread of Life* by Deacon Ken and Marie Finn, it says, "But before this time of horror and devastation comes, the faithful are to be sealed with the great seal of God so they may survive it. It is not that they escape from experiencing it, but that they may survive it." Later it says, "We see the seal of God that is placed on the forehead of the believers is the exact opposite of the mark of the beast." Could the first part of this teaching be used to fool a whole church (like the Roman Catholic Church) in the last days! I believe the Antichrist will fool them.

The Second Angel's Bowl

> *And the second angel poured out his bowl into the sea, and it became blood like that of a dead man; and every living thing in the sea died. (Rev. 16:3)*

As in the days of Moses, I believe this plague will come upon the earth.

The Third Angel's Bowl

> *And the third angel poured out his bowl into the rivers and the springs of waters; and they became blood. (Rev. 16:4)*

God turns the waters of the earth into blood because the people of the earth will try to kill all the Christians and Jews that they can find in the last days. This holocaust will be worse than the one against the Jews during World War II or the one against the religious people in Russia during Stalin's rule, which killed tens of millions of people. In Islamic prophecy, even the rocks will speak out where the Jews are hiding so that they, the Moslems, may kill them.

The Fourth Angel's Bowl

And the fourth angel poured out his bowl upon the sun; and it was given to it to scorch men with fire. And men were scorched with fierce heat; and they blasphemed God who has the power over these plagues; and they did not repent, so as to give Him glory. (Rev. 16:8-9)

Even when God is sending His wrath upon mankind in the final days of the tribulation, men will not ask God to forgive them. This fourth wrath is not the ozone above the earth disappearing but an actual burning by the sun. Sunblock number 100 will not protect you, when you go outside in those future days.

The Fifth Angel's Bowl

And the fifth angel poured out his bowl upon the throne of the beast; and his kingdom became darkened; and they gnawed their tongues because of pain, and they blasphemed the God of heaven because of their pains and their sores; and they did not repent of their deeds. (Rev. 16:10-11)

Just when you thought the sun was never going to stop burning you in the fourth bowl plague, the whole kingdom of the Antichrist becomes black. In these verses, we see the people of the earth are still in pain from their sores from the mark of the beast (666) and from the sun burning them. Yet, the people of the earth still refuse to repent to God for their sins. Maybe the people of the earth think the Antichrist is God (Rev. 13:8), and they worship his statute because they were taught in their churches that it is all right for them to pray to statues (see Exodus 20:4, 6). In the Catholic book *Trial, Tribulation & Triumph*, it says, "In the latter scenario, there is a great deal of civil war and a general war which is ended by three days of darkness. Near the end of a lengthy ensuing period of peace, things again turn bad. It might be then that the great king comes to usher in a period of peace which lasts only as long as he lives." This "great king" that the Catholic Church would like to make pope someday in the future, after he rules the whole earth, has his kingdom turn dark for three days! Does it sound like this future pope is the Antichrist or the false prophet, and that the people of his church are taught it is all right when the earth turns dark?

The Sixth Angel's Bowl

> *And the sixth angel poured out his bowl upon the great river, the Euphrates; and its water was dried up, that the way might be prepared for the kings from the east. (Rev. 16:12)*

In verse 12, the word "east" means "rising of the sun" in Greek, which means one of the countries from the East could include Japan. It also says kings (plural), which refers to more than one country from the east marching to the battle of Armageddon. This bowl of wrath sounds a lot like the sixth trumpet in Rev. 9:13-21. Although these two plagues look or sound alike, they are two different events. There is no vision here in the sixth bowl of wrath of an army of two hundred million marching from the east.

> *Behold, I am coming like a thief. Blessed is the one who stays awake and keeps his garments, lest he walk about naked and men see his shame. (Rev. 16:15)*

In verse 15, Jesus refers to Himself as a thief and reminds us to stay awake. To a person who is a post-tribulationist, this verse would show that we are not raptured out of the earth until the end of the tribulation. I believe we are raptured out of the earth before of the wrath of God in Rev. 14:16. Then, in Rev. 15:2-3, we are standing victorious in heaven worshiping God.

This verse could be referring to those left behind after the rapture because they were weak Christians that did not repent of their sins, like five of the seven churches in chapters 2 and 3 of Revelation. The parable of the ten virgins, where the five foolish ones were left behind because they had no oil, seems to match these verses below:

> *And while they (foolish virgins) were going away to make the purchase, the bridegroom came, and those who were ready went in with him to the wedding feast; and the door was shut. Later the other virgins also came, saying, "Lord, Lord, open up for us." But he answered, "Truly I say to you,*

I do not know you." Be on the alert then, for you do not know the day nor the hour. (Matt. 25:10, 13)

The Seventh Angel's Bowl

And the seventh angel poured out his bowl upon the air; and a loud voice came out of the temple from the throne, saying, "It is done." (Rev. 16:17)

It is done! With this last bowl wrath, the earth as we know it, will end. The following wrath will be very severe, and many of the people of the earth will die from it. After this last bowl wrath, Jesus Christ returns to earth to destroy the armies of the Antichrist at the battle of Armageddon so that He can set up His kingdom on earth.

And there were flashes of lighting and sounds and peals of thunder; and there was a great earthquake such as there had not been since man came to be upon the earth, so great an earthquake was it, and so mighty. And the great city was split into three parts, and the cities of the nations fell. And Babylon the great was remembered before God, to give her cup of the wine of His fierce wrath. And every island fled away, and the mountains were not found. And huge hailstones, about one hundred pounds each, came down from heaven upon men; and blasphemed God because its plague was extremely severe. (Rev. 16:18, 21)

Earlier in Revelation 6, Jesus broke the sixth seal. This seal is the same vision as the seventh bowl wrath found at the end of the tribulation.

And I looked when He broke the sixth seal, and there was a great earthquake; and the sun became black as sackcloth made of hair, and the whole moon became like blood; and the stars of the sky fell to the earth, as a fig tree casts its unripe figs when shaken by a great wind. And the sky was split apart like a scroll when it is rolled up; and every mountain and island were moved out of their places. (Rev. 6:12, 14)

Why the Wrath of God?

These are the seven bowls of the wrath of God. Mankind deserves it because they killed and tortured His saints and prophets (Rev. 16:5-6). Because of their wickedness and warped minds, these men turn on God and make war with God and the Lamb (Rev. 19:19) in the valley of the Armageddon (Rev. 16:16).

God loves us and sent His only begotten son to us so we would turn to Him. God sent prophets to His own people in the Old Testament, and the apostles and prophets to us. Yet men chose darkness over the light (Matt. 21:33-41). During the tribulation, mankind will not turn to God to ask for forgiveness of their sins, even with the two prophets in Israel prophesying and all of the last-day miracles and even in the pain of the plagues.

> *For the time will come when they will not endure sound doctrine; but wanting to have their ears tickled, they will accumulate for themselves teachers in accordance to their own desires; and will turn away their ears from the truth, and will turn aside to myths. (2 Tim. 4:3)*

Job, the prophet in the Old Testament, is our example of how to endure during times of trouble and tribulation that are coming on us in the last days.

> *Behold, we count those blessed who endured. You heard of the endurance of Job and have seen the outcome of the Lord's dealings, that the Lord is full of compassion and is merciful. (James 5:11)*

And indeed, all who desire to live godly in Christ Jesus will be persecuted. (2 Tim. 3:12)

PART 6

A REVIEW OF BABYLON'S DESTRUCTION

Chapter 17

The Harlot and the Beast

Chapter 17 is about the two mysterious creatures—the harlot and the beast—that John saw in a vision. Chapters 17 and 18 are parenthetical, as they happened earlier in Rev. 14:8; and these two chapters are a review of the events that happened to give us a greater understanding of them.

The Harlot

> *Come here, I shall show you the judgment of the great harlot who sits on many waters, with whom the kings of the earth committed acts of immorality, and those who dwell on the earth were made drunk with the wine of her immorality. (Rev. 17:1-2)*

Who is this harlot?

1. She is a great city (v. 18).
2. She reigns over the kings of the earth (v. 18).
3. This city is immoral, and the kings of the earth join her in this (v. 2).
4. She is adorned in gold and precious stones and is clothed in purple and scarlet [rich?] (v. 4).
5. She has a cup full of abominations like homosexuality, nakedness, adultery, taking the Lord's name in vain, murders, wicked planners, perversions, and so forth (Lev. 18).

6. She causes the blood of the saints, which starts during the tribulation (v. 6).

Many Bible scholars believe the information given here in chapter 17 is talking about the Roman Catholic Church, which might have been true at one time. But, what about the other churches in the world? Why couldn't they be considered as the harlot too! Some are big and rich like the Rome Catholic Church, and most Christian churches came out of her. No, Jesus is not talking about the Roman Catholic Church here because many good people in this church are saved. The Catholic Church has never promoted sexual immorality to the world, as this harlot does. In Revelation 17:18, we are told that the woman is a city and not a religion!

I believe that if Jesus Christ comes back today, there is one city and/or nation that could be represented by this harlot, and that is New York City and/or the United States (if the city is symbolic of a nation). This city might be some other city in the future, or it may have been the secular city of Rome in the past; but this vision is not talking about people's faith or a religion. Now if the oil money in the Middle East was used to rebuild the ancient city of Babylon, it could become Babylon the Great again.

> *And upon her forehead a name was written, a mystery, "BABYLON THE GREAT, THE MOTHER OF HARLOTS AND OF THE ABOMINATIONS OF THE EARTH." (Rev. 17:5)*

The Beast

> *The beast that you saw was and is not, and is about to come up out of the abyss and to go to destruction. And those who dwell on the earth will wonder, whose name has not been written in the book of life from the foundation of the world, when they see the beast, that he was and is not and will come. (Rev. 17:8)*

The beast is a charismatic world leader that is killed in the middle of the tribulation. He is going to become the Antichrist. When he gets killed, his soul goes to hell. Then Satan will bring the beast's soul out of the abyss to possess him and to rule the world. When Jesus Christ returns, the beast will go into the destruction of hell, as verse 8 writes,

> *Here is the mind which has wisdom. The seven heads are seven mountains on which the woman sits, and they are seven kings; five have fallen, one is,*

> *the other has yet to come; and when he comes, he must remain a little while. (Rev. 17:9-10)*

These verses can be hard to understand, but I think it is important to understand that these two verses are talking about world rulers, mainly from the past, and not a city set on seven hills. Most scholars believe that these seven hills in verses 9 and 10 are talking about Rome, but the city of Constantinople was built on seven hills too! The Roman Empire was the sixth kingdom, and the seventh has not come yet; but many believe it will be the European common market.

> *And the beast which was and is not, is himself also an eight, and is one of the seven, and he goes to destruction. (Rev. 17:11)*

The beast (Antichrist) is the seventh great world ruler that gets killed in the future (Rev. 13:3), but he becomes the eighth when he comes back to life.

> *Thus he said: "The fourth beast will be a fourth kingdom on the earth, which will be different all the other kingdoms, and it will devour the whole earth and tread it down and crush it. As for the ten horns, out of this kingdom ten kings will arise; and another will arise after them, and he will be different from the previous ones and will subdue three kings. And he will speak out against the Most High and wear down the saints of the Highest One, and he will intend to make alterations in times and in law; and they will be given into his hand for a times, times, and half a time." (Dan. 7:23-25)*

Daniel gives us a little more insight into the beast or Antichrist. Some scholars believe that this vision of the fourth beast is the Roman Empire, but I believe it is the kingdom of the Antichrist that will subdue three kings.

The Harlot Again

> *And he said to me, "The water which you saw where the harlot sits, are peoples and multitudes and nations and tongues. And the ten horns which you saw, and the beast, these will make her desolate and naked, and will eat her flesh and will burn her up with fire." (Rev. 17:15-16)*

The kingdom of the harlot is very rich and powerful; and it is made up of many nations and tongues of peoples, just as the United States is now.

But the beast with his ten allies will destroy her with fire in one hour (atomic weapons?) to take the leadership role of the earth. During World War II, if the United States would have not helped the allied nations, Germany and her allies could have ruled the world for a thousand years. A future Roman Empire, made up of ten powerful world leaders, will not allow the United States to stop their new world order and world domination! In Rev. 17:15-16, this great city is destroyed just like the daughter of Babylon in Isaiah 47.

> *And the woman whom you saw is the great city, which reigns over the kings of the earth. (Rev. 17:18)*

Chapter 18

Babylon the Great

This chapter is about Babylon the Great and its destruction. This destruction of Babylon by fire is a review of what happened to it during the last half of the tribulation in Revelation 14:8. Lucky for the saints or Christians that are found in that great city, they are warned to leave that city or nation in Revelation 18:4. I used to believe this verse meant that we are raptured out of Babylon before it is destroyed; but now I know it means exactly what it says, to come out of her!

> And I heard another voice from heaven, saying, "Come out of her, my people, that you may not participate in her sins and that you may not receive her plagues." (Rev. 18:4)

Many faithful Christians will go through the beast's fiery wrath and persecutions, but they are warned ahead of time before this terrible event to leave that mighty city.

> Indeed, all who desire to live godly in Christ Jesus will be persecuted. (2 Tim. 3:12)

> After these things I saw another angel coming down from heaven, having great authority, and the earth was illumined with his glory. And he cried out with a mighty voice, saying, "Fallen, fallen is Babylon the great! And she has

become a dwelling place of demons and a prison of every unclean spirit, and a prison of every unclean and hateful bird." (Rev. 18:1, 2)

I believe this is the same angel we saw in Revelation 14:8, with his announcement that Babylon the Great had been destroyed. Revelation 18 is just a review of the events that happened during the Great Tribulation before the wrath of God in chapter 16.

And the kings of the earth, who committed acts of immorality and lived sensuously with her, will weep and lament over her when they see the smoke of her burning, standing at a distance because of the fear of her torment, saying, "Woe, woe, the great city, Babylon, the strong city! For in one hour your judgment has come . . . . And the merchants of the earth weep and mourn over her, because no one buys their cargos any more." (Rev. 18:9-11)

If the Great Tribulation started today, the United States will be the only country to fit into this vision of Babylon. Here are some reasons that I feel Babylon the Great (The Great Harlot) could possibly be the United States:

1. Rev. 17:18 says, "The woman whom you saw is the great city." New York City could be this great city because of its size and wealth; the United Nations is located there; the Statue of Liberty sits there like the harlot on many waters (Rev. 17:1); and she sits like a queen and will never see mourning (Rev. 18:7). If New York City was destroyed by a large atomic weapon, it would also destroy the power grid and many other services to Washington DC, Baltimore, Philadelphia, and other cities in the northeast. But when you read all of Revelation 18, the city appears to be only symbolic of a mighty nation because no city has that much wealth and power to reign over the kings or nations of the earth (Rev. 17:18). Also, New York City's power only comes as a part of the United States.
2. The United States is the richest and most powerful nation in the world today! (Rev. 17:18 is a symbolic fit with its power.)
3. Rev. 17:2 and 19:2 say, "The great harlot who was corrupting the earth with her fornication" (immorality). Today, the whole world watches American television shows, movies, videos, magazines, books, and so forth, that are R-rated or worse. Most of these promote premarital sex and lower-than-moral standards of the whole world with murders, lack of clothing, homosexual rights, foul language,

and perversion. The Roman Catholic Church does not promote these things but becomes a victim of them!
4. The United States could and is becoming the Great Harlot by dropping its Christian heritage. Our nation was founded on Christian principles by our founding fathers and their fathers—the Pilgrims, Puritans, Quakers. Our money says, "In God We Trust." Article 1 of the constitution says, "Freedom of Religion." The Pledge of Allegiance says, "One nation under God." The Bible is not read in the public schools anymore. When the Great Tribulation begins, the United States could be forced to lead the world in persecution of Christians, making her the Great Harlot.
5. Rome is in Europe, and so is the Vatican. They are part of the European Union, which might be part of the ten-nation or ten-leader confederacy that gives the beast its power. How can Rome be destroyed when she might be part of the ten horns, and/or the false prophet (Rev. 17:16 and Rev. 13:11)?
6. No country in the world has the commerce or trade of the United States that is mentioned in Revelation 18:11-15. All the merchants of the earth will mourn if the United States is destroyed in one hour.

Many prominent men in God's church now believe the United States is the Great Harlot of Revelation. If the Lord had come back a few hundred years ago, I believe Italy or the Roman Catholic Church could have been this harlot. Many of the great Bible scholars used to believe that Rome was the Great Harlot, and many still do, even though the city of seven hills does not match with what is written in Revelation 17 and 18. Maybe in the next generation, a new Babylon will appear in Iraq. It is called a mystery in Revelation 17:5, so we must exercise patience before God! Remember:

> *I testify to everyone who hears the words of the prophecy of his book; if anyone adds to them, God shall add to him the plagues which are written in this book; and if anyone takes away from the words of the book of this prophecy, God shall take away his part from the tree of life and from the holy city, which are written in this book. (Rev. 22:18-19)*

PART 7

THE SECOND COMING AND NEW AGES

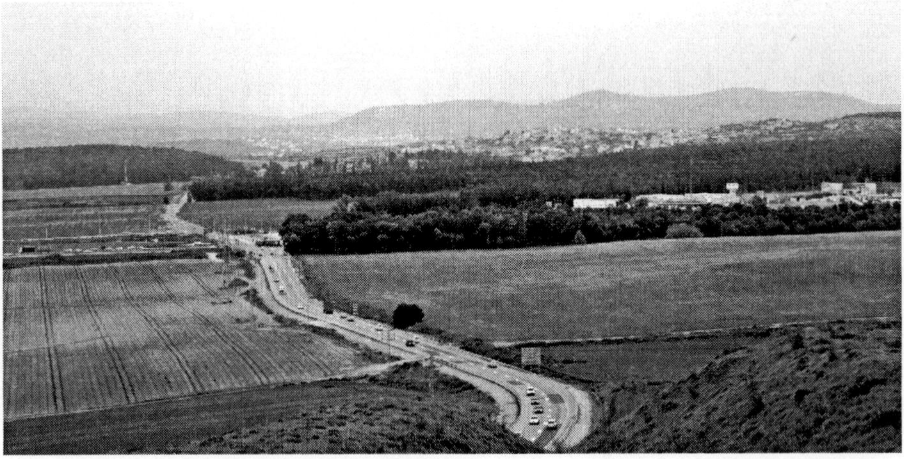

Chapter 19

The Return of Christ

Chapter 19 is talking about the return of Jesus Christ with the saints after the Great Tribulation. It can be divided into five parts:

1. The Four Hallelujahs
2. The Marriage of the Lamb
3. The Return of Jesus Christ with the Saints
4. The Birds Assemble
5. The Battle of Armageddon

The Four Hallelujahs

After these things I heard, as it were, a loud voice of a great multitude in heaven, saying, Hallelujah! Salvation and glory and power belong to our God. (Rev. 19:1)

The word "hallelujah" means praise the Lord. This first hallelujah (chorus) is from a great multitude in heaven. I believe that many in this multitude were just rescued from the earth, and they just want to thank the Lord for bringing them to heaven with many of the other saints and angels. I know that I would be praising God for my salvation and giving Him glory if I suddenly found myself in heaven at that moment. I bet that it would even sound a lot more beautiful than Handel's *Messiah*!

> *And a second time they said, "Hallelujah! Her smoke rises up forever and ever."*
> *(Rev. 19:3)*

The second "hallelujah" is praise to the Lord because the Great Harlot's smoke rises up forever! This great city or nation must have been totally corrupt and harsh to the saints during the tribulation. Her immorality and ability to harass and kill the saints could have spread through the whole world.

> *And the twenty-four elders and the four living creatures fell down and worshiped God who sits on the throne saying, "Amen. Hallelujah!"*
> *(Rev. 19:4)*

The third "hallelujah" is by the twenty-four elders and the four living creatures, as they seem to be agreeing with the great multitude in praise.

> *And a voice came from the throne, saying, "Give praise to our God, all you bondservants, you who fear Him, the small and the great." And I heard, as it were, the voice of a great multitude and as the sound of mighty peals of thunder, saying, Hallelujah! For the Lord our God, the almighty, reigns.*
> *(Rev. 19:5-6)*

The fourth "hallelujah" is the loudest because the conductor of this heavenly choir has every single bond-servant praising God. He wants everyone to give God praise because Jesus is ready to return to the earth with His bride to reign.

The Marriage of the Lamb

> *Let us rejoice and be glad and give the glory to Him, for the marriage of the Lamb has come and His bride has made herself ready.*
> *(Rev. 19:7)*

What is the meaning of this marriage? I believe it is a union of Jesus Christ with the saints in heaven. A marriage is for life, and this marriage of the Lamb (Christ) is forever with the saints. He will never leave us or forsake us (Hebrews 13:5). Hallelujah!

The Return of Christ with the Saints

And I saw heaven opened; and behold a white horse, and He who sat upon it is called Faithful and True; in righteousness He judges and wages war. And the armies which are in heaven clothed in fine linen, white and clean were following Him on white horses. And from His mouth comes a sharp sword, so that with it He may smite the nations; and He will rule them with a rod of iron; and He treads the wine press of the fierce wrath of God, the Almighty. (Rev. 19:11, 14-15)

Here you can see that Jesus Christ returns with the saints to rule the earth with an iron rod for a thousand years. But before He can rule the earth, He must finish the fierce wrath of God. As Jesus comes to earth, they will know His name that is written on Himself: "KING OF KINGS AND LORD OF LORDS" (Rev. 19:16).

The Birds Assemble

And I saw an angel standing in the sun; and he cried out with a loud voice, saying to all the birds which fly in midheaven, "Come, assemble for the great supper of God." (Rev. 19:17)

These birds will come from all over the earth to clean up the mess after the battle of Armageddon. I wonder if Alfred Hitchcock read this part of Revelation when he directed the movie *The Birds*. That movie gave me nightmares when I was a young boy. Can you imagine the look on everyone's face in Israel when Christ, the saints, and these birds are coming at the end?

The Battle of Armageddon

And I saw the beast and the kings of the earth and their armies, assembled to make war against Him who sat upon the horse, and against His army. (Rev. 19:19)

This battle isn't really a battle but a complete massacre! Here the beast, the kings of the earth, and their armies are assembled to make war against Him in Israel. Why would anyone want to even try to do battle against Jesus? Because unclean spirits performing signs will gather the armies of the whole earth to Israel for a war (Rev. 16:12-16).

> *And they gathered them together to the place which in Hebrew is called Har-Magedon. (Rev. 16:16)*

I was in the Valley of Megiddo in February of 2006, which is at the western part of the Valley of Jezreel in Northern Israel. This valley seems like the perfect place to stage the world's armies because the agricultural lands are relatively flat, and there are lots of paved roads crossing the valley. I noticed that there are numerous wells in the area and small reservoirs that could support a major army. The climate would be great for that army because it never gets too hot or too cold. I also noticed that there are airfields in the area. I feel that many of the world's Islamic countries will support this army, including the many large Moslem cities (Jenn, Nazareth, Nablus, and so forth) that surround this valley.

> *And the beast was seized, and with him the false prophet who performed the signs in his presence, by which he deceived those who had received the mark of the beast and those who worshiped his image; these two were thrown alive into the lake of fire that burns with brimstone. (Rev. 19:20)*

Remember God's Laws in the Last Days

Remember the laws and the commandments of God, and you will be blessed. The prophet Daniel warned us that many Christians or Jews would be deceived in the last days:

> *And some of those who have insight will fall, in order to refine, purge, and make them pure, until the end-time; because it is still to come at the appointed time. (Dan. 11:35)*

Today, there are people in America who call themselves Christians, and yet they walk in the ways of the world. They are into adultery, premarital sex, foul language, money, homosexuality, etc. (Jude 1:14-19). There are other Christians who are not involved with these types of sins, but they are falling for lack of knowledge of His basic commands—knowing the commandments of God.

> *You shall not make for yourself an idol, or any likeness of what is in heaven above or on the earth beneath or in the water under the earth. You shall not worship them or serve them. (Deut. 5:8)*

Many Christians who pray to statues and pictures of saints or light candles to them do not even know that they are in the wrong. Some day, they or their children may worship a statue that can speak or maybe even cry tears of blood because they were told to venerate the saints.

Biblical Prophecies about the Second Coming

> *And the rest were killed with the sword which came from the mouth of Him who sat upon the horse, and all the birds were filled with their flesh. (Rev. 19:20)*

> *Have you entered the storehouses of snow, or have you seen the storehouses of the hail, which I have reserved for the time of distress, for the day of war and battle? (Job 38:22-23)*

> *Multitudes, multitudes in the valley of decision! For the Lord is near in the valley of decision. The sun and moon grow dark, and the stars lose their brightness. (Joel 3:14-15)*

> *And in that day His feet will stand on the Mount of Olives, which is in front of Jerusalem on the east; and the Mount of Olives will be split in its middle from the east to the west by a very large valley, so that half of the mountain will move toward the north and the other half toward the south . . . Then the Lord, my God, will come, and all the holy ones with Him! (Zech. 14:4-5)*

> *But immediately after the tribulation of those days* THE SUN WILL BE DARKENED, AND THE MOON WILL NOT GIVE ITS LIGHT, AND THE STARS WILL FALL *from the sky, and the powers of the heavens will be shaken. And then the sign of the Son of Man will appear in the sky, and all the tribes of the earth will mourn, and they see the* SON OF MAN COMING ON THE CLOUDS OF THE SKY *with power and great glory. (Matt. 24:29-30)*

> *And the seventh angel poured out his bowl upon the air; and a loud voice came out of the temple from the throne, saying, "It is done . . . And there were flashes of lightning and sounds and peals of thunder; and there was a great earthquake, such as there had not been since man came to be upon the earth, so great an earthquake was it, and so mighty. And the great city was split into three parts and the cities of the nations fell . . . And every island fled away, and the mountains were not found. (Rev.16:17-20)*

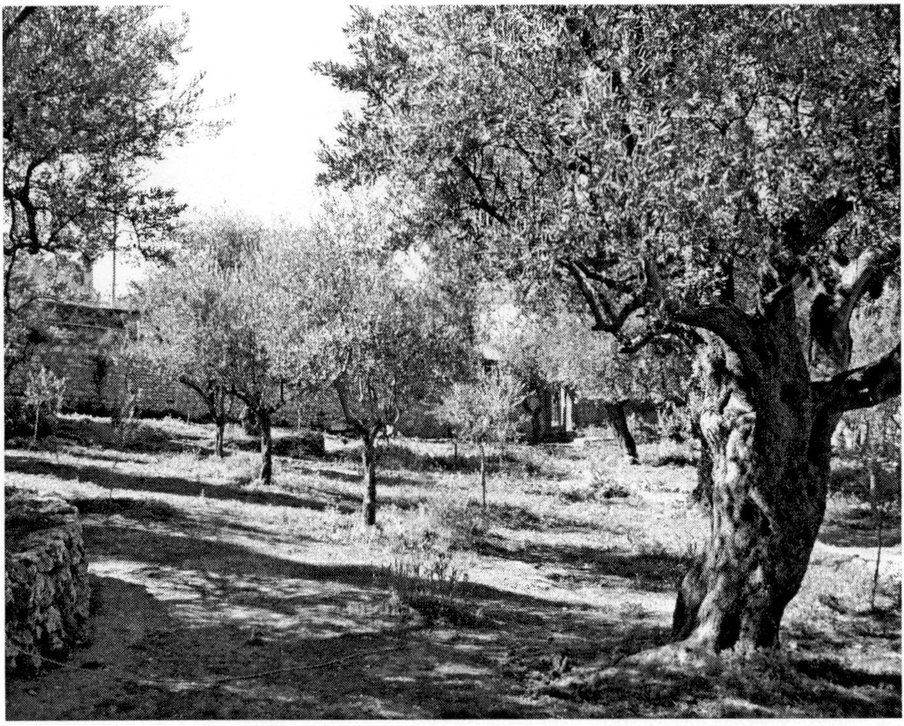

Chapter 20

The Millennium and the Judgment

This chapter is about the millennium and the judgment of mankind after the resurrection of the dead. Most people have no idea that there is a millennium coming because it is rarely mentioned in the New Testament, but they know about the coming judgment of God. The word *millennium* comes from two Latin words (mille and annus), which means "thousand year." It is a time of peace when Jesus Christ will rule over the earth from His throne in Jerusalem. After this time of peace, the final judgment of men will take place; and the old heaven and earth will be destroyed.

Satan is Bound

> *And I saw an angel coming down from heaven, having the key of the abyss and a great chain in his hand. And he laid hold of the dragon, the serpent of old, who is the devil and Satan, and bound him for a thousand years. (Rev. 20:1-2)*

In these verses, we see that Satan is bound in chains for a thousand years after having free reign on the earth for the last three and a half years. Satan is not thrown into the Lake of Fire, or hell, like the beast and the false prophet in Revelation 19:20; but Satan is going to be put into the abyss. This appears to be a spiritual holding ground (purgatory?). In Job 1 and 2, we can see that

Satan was able to go wherever he wanted to, even heaven. Now, during the millennium, his travels are limited because he is chained in the abyss. He and all of the other fallen angels, or spirits, cannot visit heaven or earth until the one-thousand-year millennium is over.

> *So it will happen in that day, that the Lord will punish the host of heaven, on high, and the kings of the earth. And they will be gathered together like prisoners in the dungeon, and will be confined in prison; and after many days they will be punished. (Isa. 24:21-22)*

The Millennium

> *And I saw thrones, and they sat upon them, and judgment was given to them. And I saw the souls of those who had been beheaded because of the testimony of Jesus and because of the word of God, and those who had not worshiped the beast or his image, and had not received the mark upon their forehead and upon their hand; and they came to life and reigned with Christ for a thousand years. (Rev. 20:4)*

The millennium is a period of one thousand years that begins right after the Great Tribulation. In Revelation 19:14-15, the armies from heaven return to earth with Jesus who will rule the earth with an iron rod. Since the saints and 144,000 bond-servants will have perfected bodies, they will not have families anymore; but they will help Jesus reign from Jerusalem. The earth will be a huge mess after about six thousand years of wars, pollution, and the wrath of God. Many Bible teachers say that only Christians can enter the millennium or that there will be no survivors on the earth; but verse 4 talks about judgments: "And I saw thrones, and they sat upon them, and judgment was given to them." So, is there anyone left on earth that can be judged worthy to enter the new age? Yes!

> *The earth will be completely laid waste and completely despoiled, for the Lord has spoken this word. Therefore, a curse devours the earth, and those who live in it are held guilty. Therefore, the inhabitants of the earth are burned and few men are left. (Isa. 24:3, 6)*

> *Then it will come about that any who are left of all the nations that went against Jerusalem will go up from year to year to worship the King, the Lord of hosts, and to celebrate the Feast of Booths. (Zech. 14:16)*

It appears from the scriptures above, and others throughout the Bible, that some people will be judged worthy to live and have their families in the millennium. Many Jewish writers of the past and present believe that people will survive the coming wrath as the writings in the Cabala show: "Happy will be all those who will remain in the world at the end of the sixth millennium to enter into [the millennium of] the Sabbath" (Zohar 1:119a).

> *Now it will come about in the last days the mountain of the house of the Lord will be established as the chief of the mountains, and will be raised above the hills; and all the nations will stream to it. And He will judge between the nations, and will render decisions for many peoples; And they will hammer their swords into plowshares and their spears into pruning hooks.... Nation will not lift up sword against nation, and never will they learn war. (Isa. 2:2, 4)*

There are mainly three different views of the millennium in Christian circles today:

1. Premillennialism—believes that Jesus Christ will come again after the tribulation to rule the earth just as the Bible teaches.
2. Amillennialism—doesn't believe there is a millennium. They spiritualize its meaning throughout the whole Bible and usually try to say we are living in that perfect spiritual world now, with Jesus Christ heading their church. (liberal and Catholic belief)
3. Postmillennialism—believes that the world will become a better and better place as time goes on, until Jesus returns and finds peace on the earth. Few people or churches believe in this view today.

The Resurrection of the Dead

> *The rest of the dead did not come to life until the thousand years were completed. This is the first resurrection. Blessed and holy is the one who has a part in the first resurrection; over these the second death has no power, but they will be priests of God and of Christ and will reign with Him for a thousand years. (Rev. 20:5-6)*

What is this first resurrection in verse 5? It is speaking of the resurrection of all Christians killed during the tribulation so that we might reign with Christ on earth. The rest of the dead that did not come to life are non-Christian or non-Jewish. I have a feeling that God has only given us a "tip of the iceberg" in prophecy here because there are dozens of other scriptures in the Old and New Testaments that deal the millennium. I think there are more mysteries in this chapter than John gave us, as the following scriptures will show:

> *Thus says the Lord, "A voice is heard in Ramah, Lamentation and bitter weeping, Rachel is weeping for her children, because they are no more." Thus says the Lord, "Restrain your voice from weeping and your eyes from tears; for your work will be rewarded," declares the Lord, and they will return from the land of the enemy. "There is hope for your future," declares the Lord, and your children will return to their own territory. (Jer. 31:15, 17)*

> *Therefore prophecy and say to them, Thus says the Lord God, "Behold, I will open your graves and cause you to come up out of your graves, My people; and I will bring you into the land of Israel." (Ezek. 37:12)*

> *For if God did not spare the natural branches, He will not spare you either. For I do not want you, brethren, to be uninformed of this mystery—so that you will not be wise in your own estimation—that a partial hardening has happened to Israel until the fullness of the Gentiles has come in; and so all Israel will be saved; just as it is written, "The Deliverer will come from Zion, He will remove ungodliness from Jacob." (Rom. 11: 21, 25-26)*

In one of the above scriptures, as Jesus returns at the Second Coming, it appears that He will cause the resurrection of the children who were killed in Bethlehem after Jesus and His family fled to Egypt. In Ezekiel 37, the bones of millions of Jews are brought back to life during the millennium. Then in Ezekiel 38 and 39, at the end of the millennium, Satan will be released to lead the armies of Gog and Magog. With the earth repopulated after one thousand years, Satan will somehow fool millions of people on the earth into following him. Then he will march on the city of Jerusalem where Christ and the saints reside.

> *When the thousand years are completed, Satan will be released from his prison, and will come out to deceive the nations which are in the four corners of the earth, Gog and Magog, to gather them together for war; the number of them is like the sand of the seashore. And they came up on the broad plain of the earth and surrounded the camp of the saints and the beloved city, and fire came down from heaven and devoured them. (Rev. 20:7, 9)*

A Great White Throne

And I saw a great white throne and Him who sat upon it, from whose presence the earth and heaven fled away, and no place was found for them. (Rev. 20:11)

When God judges mankind at the end of time, this earth and heaven will be destroyed.

And I saw the dead, the great and the small, standing before the throne, and books were opened; and another book was opened, which is the book of life; and the dead were judged from the things which were written in the books, according to their deeds. And the sea gave up the dead which were in it, and death and Hades gave up the dead which were in them; and they were judged, every one of them according to their deeds. And if anyone's name was not found in the book of life, he was thrown into the lake of fire. (Rev. 20:12-13, 15)

Yes, there is a judgment at the end of time. If we do not have faith in Jesus Christ who died for our sins and we do not repent our sins, we will not be able to enter into the new heavens and the new earth. Jesus said in John 11:25, 26a: *"I am the resurrection and the life; he who believes in me shall live even if he dies, and everyone who lives and believes in Me shall never die."*

Chapter 21

New Heaven and New Earth

As we near the end of the book of Revelation, we see a new beginning for mankind that will last forever. When I was a child, I used to ask my parents what heaven would be like, but they could never answer me. Even my catechism teachers were not sure. Here in chapter 21, we discover some of those answers about what heaven will look like and what some of our future blessings will be. Actually, eternity will not be in heaven; but it will be on the new earth because the old heaven and earth were destroyed, as we saw in Revelation 20:11.

All Things New

> *And I saw a new heaven and a new earth; for the first heaven and the first earth passed away, and there is no longer any sea. And I saw the holy city, new Jerusalem, coming down out of heaven from God. (Rev. 21:1-2)*

In these verses, we see a new heaven, a new earth, and a New Jerusalem. This new heaven and earth will be far more beautiful and spectacular than the one we live in now. Many people believe that the new earth will be like the Garden of Eden; but I believe it will be much, much more beautiful and exciting. Can you imagine a place that is more beautiful than Yosemite, the Grand Canyon, Niagara Falls, or anything else (1 Cor. 2:9)?

> *For behold, I create new heavens and a new earth; and the former things shall not be remembered or come to mind. (Isa. 65:17)*

This verse in Isaiah is telling us that the new earth is going to be so beautiful that the old one will not even come to mind. Look to see if you notice how many times in Revelation 20:11-21:1 that the earth or heaven is made new or passing away. Many people do not believe that this old earth or heaven will ever pass away; but there are many scriptures that say that it will (2 Pet. 3:7, 12-13; Heb. 12:25, 29; Rev. 21:1; Nah. 1:5, 6; Zeph.1:18; Hag. 2:6, 9).

> *And He who sits on the throne said, "Behold, I am making all things new." (Rev. 21:5)*

God Lives with Us

> *And I heard a loud voice from the throne, saying, "Behold, the tabernacle of God is among men, and He shall dwell among them, and they shall be His people, and God Himself shall be among them, and He shall wipe away every tear from their eyes; and there shall no longer be any death; and there shall no longer be any mourning, or crying, or pain; the first things have passed away." (Rev. 21:3-4)*

God is going to live with us in the future! Wow! He will not be some spirit that we cannot see: but He will be our God, and He will call us His sons (v. 7). Revelation 21:22 says that there will no longer be a temple of God, so we will not be going to church anymore—we will be the living church. Satan does not like this truth and wants people to worship him in a temple; so in the last days, he will cause the beast to rule the earth from the temple in Jerusalem. Through great miracles and lies, the beast (with Satan in him) will declare himself to be God; and if we do not worship him, he will have our heads chopped off so that he can make his false heaven on earth (Rev. 20:4). Satan is the father of lies, a false Christ, and the Abomination of Desolation (Matt. 24:15, Dan.11: 31).

The New Jerusalem

> *And he carried me away in the Spirit to a great and high mountain, and showed me the holy city, Jerusalem, coming down out of heaven from God, having the glory of God. Her brilliance was like a very costly stone, as a stone of crystal-clear jasper. (Rev. 21:10-11)*

A New Jerusalem is going to come down from heaven, glowing like a beautiful crystal jewel that is larger than the moon in total volume (Rev. 21:16). This city will be large enough to hold billions of saints from all the ages. It will be made of pure gold, giant pearls, and many other precious jewels. Her brilliance will be from the glory of God.

> *He who overcomes I will make him a pillar in . . . the New Jerusalem, which comes down out of heaven. (Rev. 3:12)*

The Twelve Foundation Stones

The twelve foundation stones of this city will have the twelve names of the apostles on them. Here are the stones and the probable rainbow of colors:

1. Jasper—reddish brown
2. Sapphire—fine blue
3. Chalcedony—sky blue with stripes
4. Emerald—bright green
5. Sardonyx—red or white
6. Sardius—fiery bloodred
7. Chrysolite—maybe golden
8. Beryl—sea green
9. Topaz—pale green to yellow
10. Chrysophase—yellow to green
11. Jacinth—violet red
12. Amethyst—purple

These stones are over 1,500 miles long and will give the city a solid foundation. They will sparkle brighter than the most beautiful of rainbows (Revelation 21:16-20). Some of you will note that five of these stones are different than the ones found on the priest's breast piece of judgment found in Exodus 28:17-20.

The Glory of God

> *And the city has no need of the sun or of the moon to shine upon it, for the glory of God has illumined it, and its lamp is the Lamb. And the nations shall walk by its light, and the kings of the earth shall bring their glory into it. (Rev. 21:23-24)*

The city will not need the sun, moon, or even electric lights to see because God will illuminate it; and the lamp will be Jesus. When Moses came down from Mount Sinai with the Ten Commandments, his face shone (glowed) from just being near God (Exod. 34:28-35).

Back in 1978, I was visiting two of the tallest buildings in the world—the World Trade Centers in New York City. The outsides of these very tall buildings were made of glass and shiny steel. That summer day, the sun reflected on them with an unusual brightness that caused everyone to appear to glow. I was amazed at the beauty of the place and the radiance that seemed to be bouncing off everyone. Maybe this is the way that the New Jerusalem is going to glow at the end of time, but much more beautifully. I hope and pray that my family and friends will be able to see this some day, but the Bible says,

> *"Only those whose names are written in the Lamb's book of life shall ever come into it"* (Rev. 21:27b).

Jesus is the Lamb of God! He died like a lamb for the forgiveness of our sins. If we repent and follow after Him, He will be faithful to bring us in to this very beautiful city.

Chapter 22

Inside Our New Home

This is the final chapter in the Bible and the book of Revelation. This chapter addresses several different topics that sometimes overlap each other:

- Inside the New Jerusalem
- Prophecies of His Quick Return
- Invitation to Be Saved
- Warning Not to Change This Book

Inside the New Jerusalem

And he showed me a river of the water of life, clear as crystal, coming from the throne of God and of the Lamb. (Rev. 22:1)

Revelation 21 shows us a little of what the new earth will be like. This chapter shows us what the inside of this beautiful new city, "The New Jerusalem" could be like on the new earth. There will be a river of life with crystal-pure water running through it, which I hope to drink from. There will be a tree of life that apparently yields a different type of fruit each month in a yearly cycle. This tree will be in the midst of a street near the throne.

And there shall no longer be any curse. (Rev. 22:3a)

One of the curses before the end of the earth was against the ground so that man had to work and sweat to produce food to eat; and to make matters worse, the ground produced thorns and thistles (Gen. 3:17-19). In the New Jerusalem, we will be able to eat and drink freely without having to work for our food, and there will always be plenty to eat.

Some people spiritualize this last chapter and claim that the river of life is figurative and not literal. Does that mean the Garden of Eden was just a figurative story (Gen. 2:8-16), or that Jesus did not go to create a new paradise with many mansions (Jn. 14:2-3)? I believe John really saw these things; and that if anyone tries to change this vision, they need to read the last four verses of this chapter.

Prophecies of His Quick Return

There are five prophecies in this chapter that refer to a quick and eminent return of Christ. Are you ready for His return?

1. *Things which must shortly take place (v. 6)*
2. *And behold, I am coming quickly (v. 7)*
3. *For the time is near (v. 10)*
4. *Behold, I am coming quickly (v. 12)*
5. *Yes, I am coming quickly (v. 20)*

John and the angel believed Christ's Second Coming was near, but it has been one thousand nine hundred years since these prophecies were told. Many teachers believe these scriptures show that Christ has already returned and has set up His kingdom on the earth, but Jesus and Paul warned us, saying,

> *But of that day and hour no one knows, not even the angels of heaven, nor the Son, but the Father alone. (Matt. 24:36)*

> *Let no one in any way deceive you, for it will not come unless the apostasy comes first, and the man of lawlessness is revealed, the son of destruction, who opposes and exalts himself above every so-called god or object of worship, so that he takes his seat in the temple of God, displaying himself as being God. (2 Thess. 2:3-4)*

Many preachers, both now and throughout history, thought the end of the world is near. All of the apostles thought that they were in the last days.

Even I believe we are nearing the end of this age, but that is just speculation. The key sign of the Second Coming of Jesus Christ is when you see the "ABOMINATION OF DESOLATION" standing in the holy place (Matt. 24:15). Then there will be "less" than three and a half years left before the rapture of the saints.

> *Truly I say to you, this generation will not pass away until all these things take place. (Matt. 24:34)*

When things start going really badly on the earth (wars, famines, floods, comets, and other natural disasters), many people believe the end is near. Some of these will be signs, but we must not lose our faith in Christ because Satan would love to see us lose our faith over Christ's delayed return.

> *Know this first of all, that in the last days mockers will come with their mocking, following their own lusts, and saying, 'Where is the promise of His Coming? For ever since the fathers fell asleep, all continues just as it was from the beginning of creation. (2 Pet. 3:3-4)*

> *But do not let this one fact escape your notice, beloved, that with the Lord, one day is a thousand years, and a thousand years is one day. The Lord is not slow about His promise, as some count slowness, but is patient toward you, not wishing for any to perish but for all to come to repentance. But the day of the Lord will come like a thief, in which the heavens will pass with a roar, and the elements will be destroyed with intense heat; and the earth and its works will be burned up. (2 Pet. 3:8-10)*

Invitation to Heaven

> *I, Jesus, have sent My angel to testify to you these things for the churches. I am the root and the offspring of David, the bright morning star. And the Spirit and the bride say, "Come." And let the one who hears say, "Come." And let the one who is thirsty Come; let the one who wishes take the water of life without cost. (Rev. 22:16-17)*

This is a beautiful invitation in verse 16 to come to Jesus now! The spirit and the bride say come! The bride in verse 17 is referring to all the people through the history of the earth that have been saved and are in heaven. They are inviting you to come to the Savior of all men, God's only begotten Son,

Jesus Christ. Jesus says if you are thirsty, which means if you want to go to heaven, and if you want to have the peace and hope right now, come to Him. Jesus said to the woman at the well in Samaria:

> *"Everyone who drinks of this water shall thirst again; but whoever drinks of the water that I shall give him shall never thirst; but the water that I shall give him shall become in him a well of water springing up to eternal life." (John 4:13-14)*

Jesus said in verse 17, "Let the one who wishes take the water of life without cost." When you come to Jesus, our Lord and Savior, you don't have to give money (10 percent), do good works, make a pilgrimage to a Mecca, visit a holy mountain or river, fast or eat only vegetables. Would the "cost" of being saved involve joining a specific church? No! Jesus said in the Gospel of John which church we needed to attend to worship Him:

> *But an hour is coming, and now is, when the true worshipers shall worship the Father in spirit and truth; for such people the Father seeks to be His worshipers. God is spirit, and those who worship Him must worship in spirit and truth. (Jn. 4:23, 24)*

So it doesn't matter which "Christian church" you belong to, as long as that church worships in the Holy Spirit and in truth. The truth which Jesus is speaking about is the Bible, which is the inspired by God (2 Tim. 3:14, 4:4).

Jesus said that unless we are born again, we could not see the kingdom of God. Being born again is accepting Jesus as your Lord and asking Him with all your heart to forgive you of your sins and to follow Him. In the book of Romans, Paul told the Christians how to be saved:

> *That if you confess with your mouth Jesus as Lord, and believe in your heart that God raised Him from the dead, you will be saved; for with the heart a person believes, resulting in righteousness, and with the mouth he confesses, resulting in salvation. (Rom. 10:9-10)*

Warning Not to Change This Book

> *I testify to everyone who hears the words of the prophecy of this book; if anyone adds to them, God shall add to him the plagues which are written in this book; and if anyone takes away from the words of the book of this prophecy,*

God shall take away his part from the tree of life and from the holy city, which are written in this book. (Rev. 22:19-20)

We are warned not to change anything in the word of God, especially in this book! That is why this warning is here! Take heed to its warning, and God will bless you when you are sharing the book of Revelation with others.

The grace of the Lord Jesus be with all. Amen. (Rev. 22:21)

Conclusion

The Prewrath Rapture Defense

I wrote this book as a simple guide to understanding the book of Revelation. But as I shared my views about the rapture of the church happening near the end of the tribulation, my Christian friends could not believe it. Would God leave His people here for the tribulation? No way would that ever happen, they would say. Even when I showed them scriptures that proved that we might be here during the tribulation, they would not listen. Below are listed seven different areas of knowledge that should help you to understand more about the real rapture. There are many more verses and pieces of information on this subject, but I feel this is enough for now.

1. Common mistakes in scripture about the pretribulation rapture
2. Where the book of Revelation shows the rapture happening
3. What the apostles taught about the rapture
4. What the earliest Christians taught about the tribulation
5. New Testament scriptures showing Christians in the tribulation
6. Saints throughout history who believed we would see the tribulation
7. Other Christian authors with similar prewrath books

1. Common Mistakes in Scripture about the Pretribulation Rapture

My fellow Christians believed that the following verses were proof from the Bible that we are raptured out of the earth before the tribulation: Titus

2:13, Revelation 4:1, Revelation 3:14, 1 Thessalonians 5:9, and Revelation 3:10. These assumptions are wrong as shown below:

The Blessed Hope. *Looking for the blessed hope and the appearing of the glory of our great God and Savior, Jesus Christ. (Titus 2:13.)* Many Bible teachers say that this verse proves that the rapture of the church takes place before the tribulation. When I read this verse, it does not mention anything about us going through the tribulation, but of a rapture possibly happening before the Second Coming. Trying to tie in the blessed hope with Christians getting raptured before the tribulation is a misuse of this scripture an assumption that is not true!

The Rapture of John in Revelation. *"Come up here, and I will show you (John) what must take place after these things." Immediately I was in the Spirit. (Rev. 4:1b, 2a)* Many Bible teachers say that this verse shows us being raptured out of the earth. This scripture is not talking about the rapture of the church, but of John going to heaven to get visions of many future events. To make a doctrine of faith on an assumption that John is the symbol of the church is not the word of God.

The "Church" Is Missing after Revelation 3:14. *"To the angel of the church in Laodicea write." (Rev. 3:14a)* Many Bible teachers say that because the word "church" is missing after the Revelation 3:14 and is not found again until after the tribulation in Revelation 22:16, this proves that the church does not go through the tribulation. This assumption, or guess, is wrong because Revelation 1:19 divides the book of Revelation into three time frames. Jesus says, *"Write therefore the things which you have seen, and the things which are, and the things which shall take place after these things."* This verse, "The things which are," is talking to the first-century church in Asia Minor. John was speaking to a specific group of churches in his time. After Revelation 4:1, John refers to the future church as saints, souls slain, ones who come out of the tribulation, offspring, etc.

Not Destined for Wrath. *And to wait for His son from heaven, whom He raised from the dead, that is Jesus who rescues us from the wrath to come. (1 Thess. 1:10)* We are not destined for the wrath of God until the sixteenth chapter of the book of Revelation. During the last part of the Great Tribulation, we see the main wrath of God. The word of God tells us very clearly that this worldwide wrath of God happens during the last part of the tribulation. The rapture of the saints is before this wrath in Revelation 14:14-16.

Keep You from That "Hour" of Testing. *"Because you have kept the word of My perseverance, I also will keep you from the hour of testing, that hour which is about to come upon the whole world, to test those who dwell on the earth." (Rev. 3:10.)* Many feel that this verse is the scriptural proof that Christians do not go through the tribulation, but this verse does not tell us when that hour of testing is going to happen. The "hour of testing" is mentioned later in Revelation 14:7: *"Fear God, and give Him glory, because the hour of His judgment has come; and worship Him who made the heaven and the earth and sea and springs of water."*

This "hour" announcement comes in the last half of the tribulation just before Babylon the Great is destroyed. During this wrath, the Christians living in that city are warned to leave it before it is destroyed. So the "hour of testing" will be at the end of the tribulation, not during the whole seven-year tribulation.

2. Where the Book of Revelation Shows the Rapture Happening

The book of Revelation actually has more then one rapture in it, but we are interested in the rapture of the church. The other raptures happen when the two witnesses of God were killed, and they were taken up to heaven at the midpoint of the tribulation (Rev. 11:12). The other rapture is the 144,000 male Jews that are the first fruits to be purchased from the earth (Rev. 14:1). The rapture of the church happens in Revelation 14, before the wrath of God in chapter 16.

> *And I looked, and behold, a white cloud, and sitting on the cloud was one like a son of man, having a golden crown on His head, and a sharp sickle in His hand. And another angel came out of the temple, crying out with a loud voice to Him who sat on the cloud, "Put in your sickle and reap, because the hour to reap has come, because the harvest of the earth is ripe." And He who sat on the cloud swung His sickle over the earth; and the earth was reaped. (Rev. 14:14-16)*

Then in Revelation 15, we see the raptured church, which came out victorious from the Great Tribulation, singing the song of Moses.

And I saw, as it were, a sea of glass mixed with fire, and those who had come off victorious from the beast and from his image and from the number of his name, standing on the sea of glass, holding harps of God. (Rev. 15:2)

3. What the Apostles Taught about the Rapture

The apostles appear to have known there was going to be some kind of rapture in the future, as indicated in these passages: Matthew 24:40-41; Matthew 25:1-13; Luke 17:43-36; 1 Thessalonians 4:13-17; and Revelations 14:14-16.

Behold, I tell you a mystery; we shall not all sleep, but we shall all be changed, in a moment, in the twinkling of an eye, at the last trumpet; for the trumpet will sound, and the dead will be raised imperishable, and we shall be charged. (1 Cor. 15:51-52)

The apostles thought they had to go through the tribulation; and according to scripture and early church history, they also thought they were near the end because of the following scriptures:

Children, it is the last hour; and just as you heard that Antichrist is coming, even now many antichrists have arisen; from this we know that it is the last hour. (1 John 2:18)

The end of all things is at hand; therefore, be of sound judgment and sober spirit for the purpose of prayer. Beloved, do not be surprised at the fiery ordeal among you, which comes upon you for your testing, as though some strange thing were happening to you. (1 Pet. 4:7-12)

Now we request you, brethren, with regard to the coming of our Lord Jesus Christ, and our gathering together to Him, that you may be quickly shaken from your composure or be disturbed either by a spirit or a message or a letter as if from us, to the effect that the day of the Lord has come. Let no one in any way deceive you, for it will not come unless the apostasy comes first, and the man of lawlessness is revealed, the son of destruction. (2 Thess. 2:1-3)

Then they will deliver you to tribulation, and will kill you. (Matt. 24:9a)

For those days will be a time of tribulation such as has not occurred since the beginning . . . . Unless the Lord had shorted those days, no life would have been saved; but for the sake of the elect. (Mk. 13:19-20) It was also given to him to make war with the saints and to overcome them, and authority over every tribe and people and tongue and nation was given to him. (Rev. 13:7)

4. What the Earliest Christians Taught about the Tribulation

The early church believed that they had to go through the tribulation. Almost all Bible scholars know that the early church fathers believed that the church would go into the tribulation. This fact can be checked by reading the hundreds of letters and books written in the first few centuries of the church. Here is a partial list of some of the more famous early Christian writers that were not pretribulationists at all: Polycarp (c. 69-156), Justin Martyr (c. 100-165), Barnabas (c. 70-100), Papias (c. 60-130), Clement of Rome (c. first century), Tertullian (c. 160-230), Ignatius (c. 35-107), Irenaeus (c. 130-200), Hippolytus (c. 170-200), Lactantius (250-325), and so forth.

If none of the early church fathers believed in a rapture of the church coming before the tribulation, why do so many fundamentalists believe in it today?

5. New Testament Scriptures Showing Christians in the Tribulation

Matthew	24:9	deliver you to tribulation
	24:10	many will fall away
	24:11	will mislead many
	4:13	one who endures to the end
	24:15	when you see the Abomination
	24:22	for the sake of the elect
	24:24	mislead . . . the elect
	24:33	when you see all these things
Mark	13:9	for they will deliver you to the courts
	13:13	you will be hated
	13:14	when you see the Abomination
	13:20	but for the sake of the elect
	13:29	when you see these happen
Luke	21:16	but you will be delivered up
	21:17	you will be hated
	21:20	when you see Jerusalem surrounded
	21:28	lift up your heads
	21:36	you may have the strength to escape
John	6:40	I Myself will raise him up on the last day
Acts	14:22	through many tribulations we must enter

Romans	5:3	exult in our tribulations . . . brings perseverance
1 Corinthians	15:52	at the last trumpet . . . the dead will be raised
2 Thessalonians	2:2-3	unless the apostasy and the man of lawlessness
James	1:12	blessed is a man who perseveres under trial
1 Peter	1:6-7	distressed by various trials . . . tested by fire
1 Peter	4:12-13	do not be surprised at the fiery ordeal . . . testing
1 Peter	5:10	and after you have suffered for a little while
1 John	2:18	Antichrists have risen . . . it is the last hour
Revelation	1:9	fellow partaker in the tribulation
	6:9-11	souls of those who had been slain during the tribulation
	7:14	who come out of the Great Tribulation
	12:17	make war with her offspring
	13:7	make war with the saints and overcome them
	14:4	purchased from among men as first fruits to God
	14:14-16	the harvest of the earth (rapture)
	15:2	those who . . . victorious from the beast

6. Saints throughout History Who Believed We Would See the Tribulation

Moses (Deut. 4:30), Job (14:13-14), David (Ps. 18:6-19), Isaiah (Isa. 26:19-21, 33:2), Daniel (Dan. 7:21-25), Joel (Joel 2:31-32), Micah (Mic. 7:6-10), Jesus (Matt. 24:15-25), the Apostles (see above, number 5), the early Christian Church (see above, number 4), Martin Luther, John Knox, John Wesley, Charles W. Spurgeon, Walter Martin, William Tyndale, A. H. Strong, George Whitfield, John Huss, William Booth, Robert H. Gundry, Matthew Henry, John Calvin, Jonathan Edwards, Isaac Newton, Morgan Edwards, Dave MacPherson, Dale Moody, Gary North, John Foxe, Dr. Campbell Morgan, William G. Moorehead, Henry G. Weston, Dr. George E. Ladd, Dr. Gleason L Archer Jr., Dr. Douglas J. Moo, and so on.

7. Other Christian Authors with Similar Prewrath Books

Peter Jurieu, *Approaching Deliverance of the Church,* 1687
Marvin Rosenthal, *The Pre-Wrath Rapture of the Church,* Thomas Nelson Publishers, 1990
Robert Van Kampen, *The Sign,* Crossway Books, a division of Good News Publishers, 1992
Jack Hayford, *E-Quake,* Thomas Nelson Publishers, 1999

The Seven Blessings of Revelation

"Blessed is he who reads and those who hear the words of the prophecy, and heed the things which are written in it; for the time is near." Rev. 1:3

"'. . . Blessed are the dead who die in the Lord from now on!' "Yes," says the Spirit, "so that they may rest from their labors, for their deeds follow with them." Rev. 14:13b

"Behold, I am coming like a thief. Blessed is the one who stays awake and keeps his clothes, so that he will not walk naked and men will not see his shame." Rev. 16: 15

"Then he said to me, 'Write, 'Blessed are those who are invited to the marriage supper of the Lamb.'" And he said to me, 'These are the true words of God.' Rev. 19: 9

"Blessed and holy is the one who has a part in the first resurrection; over these the second death has no power, but they will be priests of God and of Christ and will reign with Him for a thousand years." Rev. 20:6

"And behold, I am coming quickly. Blessed is he who heeds the words of the prophecy of this book." Rev. 22:7

"Blessed are those who wash their robes, so that they may have the right to the tree of life, and may enter by the gates into the city." Rev. 22:14

Bibliography

Bercot, David W., ed. *Dictionary of Early Christian Beliefs*. Third Printing. Peabody: Hendrickson Publishers, Inc., 2000.

Birch, Desmond A. *Trial, Tribulation & Triumph Before, During, and After Antichrist*. Santa Barbara: Queenship Publishing Co., 1996.

Couch, Mal, ed. *Dictionary of Premillenial Theology*. Grand Rapids: Kregel Publications, 1996.

Dake, Finis Jennings. *Revelation Expounded*. Tenth Printing. Lawrenceville: Dake Bible Sales, Inc., 1991.

Draper, Richard D. *Opening the Seven Seals, The Visions of John The Revelator*. Salt Lake City: Deseret Book Company, 1991.

Finn, Ken and Marie. *The Bread of Life Catholic Bible Study Cycle C*. Santa Barbara: Queenship Publishing, 1991.

Hall, Stuart G. *Doctrine and Practice in the Early Church*. Grand Rapids: Eerdmans Publishing Company, 1994.

Hayford, Jack. *E-Quake*. Nashville: Thomas Nelson, Inc., 1999.

Kimball, William R. *The Rapture*. Grand Rapids: Baker Book House, 1985.

Kirban, Salem. *666*. Wheaton: Tyndale House Publishers, 1970.

Lindsey, Hal. *The Late, Great Planet Earth*. Grand Rapids: Zondervan Publishing House, 1970.

McGee, J. Vernon. *Thru the Bible Commentary Series Revelation Chapters 1-5*. Thru the Bible Radio. Nashville: Thomas Nelson, Inc., 1991.

McGee, J. Vernon *Thru the Bible Commentary Series Revelation Chapters 6-13*. Thru the Bible Radio. Nashville: Thomas Nelson, Inc., 1991.

McGee, J. Vernon *Thru the Bible Commentary Series Revelation Chapters 14-22*. Thru the Bible Radio. Nashville: Thomas Nelson, Inc., 1991.

Rosenthal, Marvin J. *The Pre-Wrath Rapture of the Church, A New Understanding of the Rapture, the Tribulation, and the Second Coming*. Nashville: Thomas Nelson, Inc., 1990.

Van Kampen, Robert. *The Sign*. Wheaton: Crossway Books, 1992.

Watch Tower Bible and Tract Society of Pennsylvania. *Revelation: Its Grand Climax At Hand!* New York: Watchtower Bible and Tract Society of New York, Inc., 1988.